CUSTOMER SERVICE

A How-To-Do-It Manual
For Librarians

Suzanne Walters

HOW-TO-DO-IT MANUALS
FOR LIBRARIANS

Number 41

NEAL-SCHUMAN PUBLISHERS, INC.
New York, London

I owe special thanks to the Denver public Library and Salt Lake City Public Library for the assistance in preparing this book. And to Rick Ashton and the staff and customers of the Denver Public Library, I'd like to express special appreciation. DPL's customer service programs helped the library achieve a $91.6 million bond election victory. They serve as an example and as continuing inspiration for me.

Published by Neal-Schuman Publishers, Inc.
100 Varick Street
New York, NY 10013

Z
711
.W275
1994

Copyright © 1994 by Suzanne Walters

Printed and bound in the United States of America

Library of Congress Cataloging-in-Publication Data

Walters , Suzanne.
   Customer service : how - to - do - it manual for librarians / Suzanne Walters
      p.   cm. - - (How - to - do - it manual for librarians : no. 41)
   Includes bibliographical references and index.
   ISBN 1-55570-137-X :
   1. Libraries and readers -- United States .   2. Customer service -
- United States.   I. Title.   II. Series : How - to - do- it manuals for
libraries :   no. 41.
Z711 . W275   1994
025 .5 -- dc20
                                   94 - 6277
                                       CIP

CONTENTS

1 WHY DO WE NEED GOOD CUSTOMER SERVICE?

Why do we need good customer service? Good customer service creates satisfied customers who come back again and again. Beyond that, good service will result in customers voting for bond elections, contributing private dollars, and volunteering to support libraries. Poor customer service will result in lost elections and lost funding. It is as simple as that. Good customer service pays

Customer expectations have increased. We have been educated by the service providers, such as McDonald's restaurants, Nordstrom, and Federal Express. We expect libraries will provide the same level of service as other service industries. And these service expectations will continue to grow, as customers continue to become more knowledgeable.

The Library customer is more sophisticated, demanding, and educated than ever before. This customer has alternatives. If libraries are to survive and thrive, they must realize that they are there to meet the needs of their customers and communities. Libraries cannot afford to simply be warehouses for information. In this scenario, libraries have the information, and customers are expected to find it themselves. That scenario simply won't work as information sources become more diversified and complex. Libraries must reach out and meet specific customer information needs that librarians need to serve customers even more personally.

As the information business changes, our customer will have greater choices. Cable television and telecommunications companies are merging to deliver information directly to the home or business. Libraries will be changed in this process, too. We will be delivering more and more information electronically. The library must offer the "value-added" element of service. This element can set libraries apart in the competitive market place. As libraries become the facilitator for information access for customers, and as they introduce the new technology to customers, that element of service will give them the competitive edge.

A library that provides good customer service is a fun place to work. the morale and enthusiasm of employees is high. Employees pass this enthusiasm on to customers. Those employees also provide a much more stable work force. Absenteeism is reduced or eliminated. Employees feel like they can make a decision, and that they can be trusted. They also feel like they are important members of a team. The workplace climate moves away from us vs. them.

THE HIGH COST OF AN UNHAPPY CUSTOMER

The majority of unhappy customers never complain. In fact, 96 percent of the customers never complain about rude or discourteous treatment. But 90 percent of those customer who are dissatisfied with the service they receive will not come back. Each one of those unhappy customer will tell his or her story to at least nine other people. Thirteen percent of those unhappy former customers will tell their stories to more than 20 people. (This information comes from a study conducted for the White House Office of Consumer Affairs by TARP, a Washington, D.C. consultant.)

Most businesses find that 20 percent of their customers account for 80 percent of their business. When one of these customers is lost, it makes a substantial difference in the business activity. In libraries, too, 20 percent of our customers account for 80 percent of the business. These 20 percent are strong advocates of libraries. A loss of one of these customers makes an impact.

It costs six times as much to get a new customer as it does to retain an old one. It costs six times as much to get a new donor than it does to keep an old one. This cost represents advertising, special programs, and library card sign-up events.

In the environment of consumer goods, you can actually put a price on the value of customer loyalty. The automobile industry believes that a loyal customer represents a lifetime average revenue of $140,000. The local supermarkets believe that their average customer spends $4,400 in one year.

50,000 MOMENTS OF TRUTH

In 1981, Scandinavian Airlines System (SAS) was struggling with a downturn in business. The world wide recession at the time cut into all airlines' profits. A young man, Jan Carlson, was offered the position of president of SAS. He was flamboyant and energetic with a strong background in marketing. He embarked on an all out campaign to turn the airline around. He based his strategy on a simple marketing philosophy: Give the customer what he wants!

He preached customer service. He had employees keeping tabs on customers at each stage they dealt with the airline. He undertook training programs for all of the front-line staff at every location of SAS. He knew that the new concept would require a radical redirection of the thoughts and energies of everyone in the organization. He realized that it would take too much time to simply work with the managerial group of the airline. He went directly to the 20,000 employees in three countries. He formed teams of consultants and managers. He and his executives personally became evangelists.

As you know, all of this effort paid off. There was a spectacular turnaround for SAS. The airline went from a $8 million loss to a gross profit of $71 million on sales of $2 billion in a little over a year.

"We have 50,000 moments of truth out there everyday," said Jan Carlson. He was referring to each point at which a customer comes into contact with any part of the company. At each point, the customer forms an opinion of the airline.

Libraries function in the same way. There are 50,000 moments of truth each day. Even though that particular number may be too large for a library, the same philosophy holds true. Every contact a customer makes within the library is an opportunity for the customer to form an opinion. Calling the library, signing up for a library card, and looking for material are all interactions that allow the customer to form an opinion. They carry their opinion to the ballot box, to the City Council, as well as to their friends and neighbors.

When the "moments of truth" go unmanaged, the quality of service regresses to mediocrity.

The quality of service should be considered as a triangle with the customer in the middle. First of all, there needs to be a service strategy, the systems need to be customer oriented, and the people need to provide the human touch.

WHAT ARE THE MAJOR BARRIERS TO GOOD CUSTOMER SERVICE?

The differences in people. Most people are not sensitized to customers. It takes training and support to make the cultural change and create a sensitivity to customers.

Customer service requires that front-line staff use their "informed judgement" with customers all the time. Training and support are needed before front-line staff will feel comfortable doing this. It is much safer to have a "rule book" upon which to rely.

When establishing a customer service program in the library, realize that the 80/20 rule will apply once again. Approximately 20 percent of your employees will embrace new customer service strategies. The other 80 percent may resist. The 20 percent become your champions who will lead the change by example. They must be rewarded if the change is to be complete.

Many long-term employees may be very resistant to change. In fact, some of them don't realize that they are offensive to customers. This resistance poses problems for the library. Managers and supervisors must have adequate training to be able to handle these situations successfully.

Customer Service is a long-term commitment for any organization. This commitment must be reflected in hiring practices. New employees selected need to have customer service skills even if they are working in support functions.

Believing that customers are expendable. "This would be a great job, except the customers keep messing up the books!" Some customers are difficult, but they are not expendable. After all, the reason we need libraries is to help people get the information they need.

Unwillingness to pay the price. What is the price? The price is training and retraining. It is new reward and recognition programs. It is the ongoing commitment to quality.

Budgetary problems are real, of course. Often we say that we cannot provide good service because we can't hire the staff or buy the materials. The budget must be examined in view of customer service and priorities need to be changed. It is important to do some things really well, rather than provide more programs and services poorly. Priorities must be set. Understand who your primary customers are and provide them with good customer service.

Customer service is never finished. There is no such thing as a "completed" customer service program. This service mandate requires constant vigilance. It is a short term revolution and a long term commitment.

Superficial commitments. It takes organization-wide commitment to customer service to make it work. In any library with more than two people, there is a chain of service. As the saying goes, the chain is only as strong as its weakest link. Each function in the library must be committed to customer service or the entire process can break down.

Organizations that simply put "buttons" on the employees and banners in the hall are making a superficial commitment.

Listening but not hearing, looking but not seeing. It is easy to get caught up in the deadlines and demands of the library. We simply come in the front door and head for the office to write reports or complete projects. We don't take the time to really listen and watch customers. Yet each customer's perspective is new and unique. If we will listen, our customers will ask the questions that we need to know. The search for directions, for change, for materials lets us know where we need to improve.

All of the service superstars have managers who "walk about" and mingle with the customers. This "walking about" needs to be done in an informal way. An announced visit by management personnel does not provide the opportunity for spontaneity and close interaction with the customers.

Invite customers to come in and talk to you. Ask them if they found what they were looking for. Listen to them. Children, too, have concerns over customer service. They are sometimes so articulate and direct. They can provide you with invaluable insight.

Looking and listening becomes everybody's job. Encourage the ability to look and listen by setting the example. Talk about what you heard and saw at staff meetings.

FIGURE 1-1: Barriers In Your Library

What are the barriers to developing a customer service program in your library?

1. Lack of staff training?

2. Believing that the customer is expendable?

3. Policies and procedures that create an unfriendly customer atmosphere?

4. Determining how to measure good customer service?

5. Unwillingness to pay the price?

Quality service is hard to define and measure. What is quality service in a library? It means different things to different people at different times.

Performance standards need to be established so that service can be measured. For example, a 24-hour turnaround on books and materials in the system. A specific response rate to reference questions may be yet another example. Survey the customers to understand the service standards that are important to them.

Policies and procedures—"we've always done it this way!" There are few experiences that are more frustrating to a customer than being told, "It's our policy, I can't do anything about it!" Policy and procedure manuals and computer systems take on a life of their own within organizations. Somehow, they weaken able bodied intelligent employees into submission.

Employees need guidance. Customer service training enables employees to make judgemental decisions on the front line that are in opposition to stated policies. Have policies been developed so that staff don't have to think?

In a service orientation, policies need to be reconsidered. Flexibility becomes the rule. Only through constant training will the staff be comfortable about using their "informed judgement."

Selling what you cannot deliver. If you promote free balloons for all the children participating in the summer reading program and run out of balloons, you have made children and their parents very upset.

Do a few things really well. Promote the things you do well. Don't promote services or programs that you can't deliver.

THE DEMANDS OF QUALITY SERVICE

This is not an exhaustive list of barriers, by any means. There are many more. The bottom line is that it is difficult to develop quality service programs. It is equally hard to maintain them.

FIGURE 1-2: Exercise Looking and Listening

Exercise:

Stand in the middle of the floor with your library name tag on. See how much easier it is for customers to approach you and ask questions. Ask customers if they found what they needed.

Quality service requires constant vigilance, training, and commitment. It demands the following:

Changing the culture

Staff within libraries feel like they are providing good customer service. There are traditional ways of dealing with customers. Policies and procedures have been in place for a long time. It is difficult, often, to create an awareness that we need to change. In addition, the actual change in culture does not come easily. This cultural change must be demonstrated, rewarded, and encouraged.

Creating a risk-taking environment

Libraries have been bureaucratic in design. They have not encouraged risk taking. Customer service requires more authority by line staff. Staff members must be given the information with which to make decisions on the spot. They must be trained to provide the customer with good service, even when there is a conflict with policy. This requires the ability to take the risk of being wrong. There will be mistakes. Employees need to know if they make a mistake they won't lose their job.

Developing informed judgement

Rules, policies, and accepted procedures are often convenient to hide behind. In a customer-oriented environment, we expect line staff to make decisions and to use their judgement. But they require training and support to do this. They also need access to good information in order to feel informed.

Delegating

Trusting employees to make the right decisions and allow them to try. Delegation of responsibility is required in a customer orientation. Managers need to delegate decisions regarding customers to line staff. That is often difficult for them to do.

Providing autonomy and trust

Creating an environment in which an individual employee can make a mistake is important. Creating an atmosphere of trust and autonomy enables employees to feel important and respected. These employees will provide the best service to customers.

Developing a reward system with incentives

If we are going to change the culture, we must have rewards that recognize positive behavior. The rewards stimulate all employees to seek positive reinforcement in this manner.

Creating systems of accountability

Systems of accountability must be established. They can be set up through changes in job descriptions and evaluation forms that evaluate for levels of customer service. Both reward systems and systems for reprimanding employees who are not providing good service serve as methods of accountability. Accountability is the method by which the organization puts the "teeth" in its customer service program.

The impact of leadership

The library director sets the example for customer service for every staff member. Employees are all customers of the library director. Employees will treat customers the way they are treated by the library director.

2 EXAMPLES OF GOOD CUSTOMER SERVICE

Some corporations are well known for their customer service. In fact, their level of customer service has made them distinctive as well as highly successful. These companies demonstrate how important service has been to them in their business and what a difference it has made.

FEDERAL EXPRESS

"Absolutely Anywhere overnight!" This motto signifies the commitment Federal Express makes to its customers. The company has been known to hire a Lear Jet to deliver a package overnight.

Federal Express agents receive five weeks of up-front training: two weeks on the job, two weeks of classroom instruction that details the operational requirements, and one week on the job to utilize what they learned. Then they must pass a final test.

Federal Express operates on a hub system. Packages are delivered to one hub, and then sent on to various locations throughout the United States. Can you just imagine how many millions of dollars it invested in this concept? It was new, risky, and innovative.

FIGURE 2-1: **Federal Express**

Federal Express delivers absolutely anywhere, overnight? Can your library also deliver absolutely anywhere overnight?

What changes would you have to make to provide this kind of delivery service?

L.L. BEAN

In 1912, L.L. Bean, a Maine hunter and fisherman, created the Maine Hunting Shoe. This shoe consisted of a rubber bottom and a leather top. He obtained a list of people living outside of Maine who had purchased a fishing license in the state. He sent them all a brochure advertising his new boots. He received and filled 100 orders. However, 90 of the boots were returned because the stitching between the tops and the bottoms did not hold. Bean refunded the customers' money and took out a loan to improve the design of the boots.

Today the Maine Hunting Shoe is L.L. Bean Company's core product. The company still stands behind its 100 percent satisfaction-guaranteed policy.

The L.L. Bean philosophy is, "Sell good merchandise at a reasonable profit, treat your customers like human beings and they will always come back for more."

Customer service is dealing with customers one call at a time, one letter at a time. It is paying attention to the details. L.L. Bean pays attention to complaints. In fact, it has an 800 number to encourage customers to call.

Employees go the extra mile for the customer. An example of the quality of its service is visible in this story: A customer ordered a jacket for a friend who was going into the hospital. The jacket was out of stock. However, a recent catalogue said the jacket was being promoted as a special. The customer called up in anger and demanded the jacket, as it had been specially advertised. An employee went to the distribution center and found the exact jacket that the customer wanted. (It had been returned by another customer but not yet placed back in the inventory system.) The employee sent the jacket on an express flight to New York City, and had a limo take it from there to the customer's house, in time for him to give it to his friend.

Corporations and organizations who stick to their core values are successful. In the case of L.L. Bean, the core value is to provide each customer with a 100 percent guarantee policy for goods purchased.

WALT DISNEY WORLD

This is the place that makes dreams come true. Every customer is a "guest" and a VIP. Every staff member is on stage. Every one has a vital role in preparing for the show, whether it is cleaning bathrooms, handling parking, or guiding a tour. Employees are also taught from the beginning that guests should be treated equally.

Hiring the best and training them right are critical to Walt Disney World: The process begins during the interviewing process. Management looks for people who are willing and able to work in any area of guest relations. They look for individuals who are enthusiastic and self-confident.

The training begins immediately after being hired. New employees learn about the Disney company and the facilities. They learn about office locations, bathroom locations, telephones, and food facilities. Then they begin a two-month program of daily job rotations. They are rotated daily to different parts of Walt Disney World.

The bottom line is that guests go home with a feeling that they are VIP's. It's the attitude about customers that makes this organization so well known all around the world for the excellence of its service.

FIGURE 2-2: What kind of orientation do you have for your team members?

1. Tours of facilities?

2. Job rotation and cross-training?

3. Background sessions, including introductions of new employees to key personnel?

4. Discussions of the mission, vision, and strategic plans of the library?

5. Functions and activities to support and encourage teambuilding?

MCDONALD'S RESTAURANTS

There are more than 15,000 McDonald's restaurants in 50 countries. Each day, millions of customers are greeted cheerfully and sincerely by McDonald's employees. Remember that these are minimum wage employees ranging in age from 17 to 70. Most of them are part time workers, and receive no benefits or tips. How does McDonald's do it?

Yes, they spend millions of dollars on advertising and sales promotion each year. However, the reason for their good service is McDonald's meticulous attention to detail. It is an operation-oriented company. That may not be visible from the customer point of view.

But McDonald's commitment to service and to good human resource management begins at the top corporate level. This commitment is promoted in all of its regions, districts, offices, and every facility and restaurant.

Hamburger University operated by McDonald's has received world recognition for training young entrepreneurs from foreign countries.

You can count on the same high level of service at every McDonald's. Is that true of your library?

McDonald's french fries are of the same quality and consistency throughout every location in the country. Franchisees must adhere to quality standards. Do you have quality standards in your library? Do branches or departments adhere to those standards?

FIGURE 2-3: **You can count on the same high level of service at every McDonald's. Is that true of your library?**

McDonald's french fries are of the same quality and consistency at every location in the country. Franchisees must adhere to quality standards. Do you have quality standards in your Library? Do branches or departments adhere to those standards?

WHAT DO THE SERVICE ROLE MODEL COMPANIES HAVE IN COMMON?

What management policies and values do they share? It is possible to distill nine characteristics that these companies share:

1. Each of the companies is headed by a leader who vehemently believes in customer service. These leaders "walk about." They mix with customers, they set the standards and the expectations.

2. These companies all recognize that employee relations mirror customer relations. If they are to be superior in customer service, they realize that they have to be superior in relationships with their employees.

3. Each of these companies creates an awareness of the importance of customer service in the minds of their employees. Employees are taught that the customer is the ultimate.

4. Each of the companies has developed and implemented support systems to teach and reinforce the expected behavior.

5. The companies define and implement precise and demanding performance standards. They couple these standards with high performance expectations.

6. They train and retrain managers, supervisors, and employees to reinforce and maintain desired behaviors.

7. The companies provide tangible and intangible recognition and rewards for achievement and customer service. They make employees feel appreciated.

8. They use quantitative measures to monitor effectiveness. They use quantitative measures not only in the area of sales, but in personnel policies, practices, and procedures.

9. These companies build in strong, continuing reinforcement to sustain the customer-oriented systems. They build a "corporate culture" based on service.

3 CUSTOMER SERVICE IN A MARKETING FRAMEWORK

Libraries have begun to embrace marketing's principle of understanding who their customers are and what those customers want. Information includes segmentation, competition, demand as well as product, price, promotion, and place. Market research provides the data through which the appropriate marketing strategy can be developed.

In the process of developing customer service programs we are developing an internal marketing program. This internal marketing program refers to the set of programs, strategies, and activities designed to understand and motivate employees within the organization. Service firms, including libraries, know that they must first sell the firm to the employees so that the employees can sell the firm (or library) to the customers.

Customer service demands that we understand our employees as customers. We have to develop an awareness that our employees are customers, too. This consciousness will be developed through some of the same tools we use in traditional marketing programs. Market research, internal marketing communication programs, hiring processes, training, and accountability are all useful tools in this internal marketing process.

This internal marketing effort determines the quality of the customer's experience in the library. Every employee makes a difference in the customers' perception of the quality of their experience at the library. Customers will perceive the library as a high-quality organization if their experiences match their expectations. If those experiences are positive, these customers become advocates of the library. In these days of funding issues, libraries need all of the advocates that they can get.

WHO ARE THE CUSTOMERS?

Traditionally we think of the library's customers as those individuals and groups who come to the library for books, programs and materials. These customers or users of the library represent a wide base. In addition to those traditional customers, there are additional stockholders in the library who should be considered "customers." All of these customers should be considered as targets for our service excellence program.

THE LIBRARY'S PUBLICS OR CUSTOMERS

EMPLOYEES
- Managers
- Clerical staff
- Professional staff
- Retired employees
- New employees
- Outstanding employees

THE LIBRARY'S FUNDERS
- Public funding sources
- City council
- City manager
- Mayor
- Elected officials
- City budgeting office
- State Legislators
- Politicians running for office, politicians with a "stake"
- The electorate

PRIVATE FUNDING SOURCES
- Corporations
- Foundations
- Individuals

THE MEDIA
- General press
- Business press
- Library press
- Wire services

- Electronic media
- Friendly journalists
- Hostile journalists
- Local Weekly publications
- Community publications
- Business newsletters

LIBRARY CUSTOMERS

- Satisfied customers
- Dissatisfied customers
- New customers
- Old customers
- Potential customers
- Customers in segments
  - Children
  - Minorities
  - Elderly
  - Special interest groups
  - Neighborhoods
  - Students
  - Educators
  - Community groups

Employees are the ones who actually deliver the services of any library to the customers. Those employees need to fully understand the services and the expectations of them, or else the intended services will never reach the customer. We need to communicate not only to the external customer, but to the internal ones as well.

Customers evaluate their library experience based on a number of key components. Problems with any of the components create customer service issues. Those components include the following:

1. Environment: Physical environment refers to the physical structure of the building, the parking facilities, and to the care of the buildings. Are the buildings dirty? Are the

restrooms dirty? Are there adequate places to read or study? Is the lighting adequate? Are the buildings safe?

2. Systems: Systems can include the automated card catalogue, the process through which one gets a library card, the delivery system, and systems to provide copies of needed material. Do your typewriters work? Copy machines work? Are there long lines to check out materials? What kind of renewal system do you have? Is the equipment up to date? What kind of systems are in place to deliver information? Are they cumbersome or slow? Libraries cannot be all things to all people. Does your library have adequate systems in place to get the information your customers want?

3. Amenities: Literacy programs, community programs, book clubs, story hours, publications that provide directions or the book list you need, signage, bulletin boards, newsletters, book reviews—all of the things that enable you to find your way around the library and maximize your use of the library.

4. People Skills: Technical competence is needed within the library environment. However, more than technical competence is required in providing good customer service. People skills have a dramatic impact on customer satisfaction.

Implementing a customer service program requires a cultural change within the organization. It requires examining systems and equipment, environment, and amenities. It also requires the development of people skills and consciousness-raising concerning the importance of customers.

FIGURE 3-1: How Does Your Library Rate in the Following Areas?

Customer Service

1. Environment (facilities, buildings)

2. Systems (equipment, automated card catalog)

3. Amenities (signage, publications, programs)

4. People skills

4 MANAGEMENT PHILOSOPHY AND COMMITMENT

The key to success in the development of a customer service oriented workforce lies with the library director. It is the library director who sets the example of leadership, of commitment to his/her customers both internal (employees) and external. This leadership must be focused with the managers and administrators who work with the employees on a daily basis. "The dominant principle of organization has shifted, from management in order to control an enterprise to leadership in order to bring out the best in people and to respond quickly to change," said John Naisbitt in Megatrends 2000.

Many managers have been "short-term, control-oriented, report oriented," says Russell E. Palmer, former dean of the University of Pennsylvania's Wharton School of Business. "Leaders think longer term, grasp the relationship of larger realities, think in terms of renewal, have political skills, cause change, affirm values and achieve unity." "Leaders recognize that while capital and technology are important resources, people make or break a company. Leaders inspire commitment and empower people by sharing authority."

The essential ingredient for a successful customer service program lies in the leadership and management philosophy of the organization.

Management gurus Tom Peters (author of *In Search of Excellence*) and Clay Sherman (author of *The Uncommon Leader*) articulate the importance of leadership. Peters speaks of the need for "organizational champions" who are value-driven, and the value that drives them is service. Those leaders stay close to the customer. "They are sticklers for detail, they spend money on quality. They manage by walking around, and they make the typical employee a hero. Successful leaders in organizations with good customer service realize that they can't do it all themselves. They empower people. They build teams. They give credit. They have one standard and one standard alone: excellence."

Sherman talks of Sam Walton who was one of the richest men in the country. He spearheaded Walmart Stores. Sam used to visit each one of his 700 stores annually. His formula was simple: "Listen to the customer. Believe what they tell you. Do what they tell you to do."

Developing library organizational champions and leaders is the strategy for service excellence in the library. To achieve these ends, library directors and managers need to practice the following six principles:

1. *Preach and lead with vision.* The library director and the management team need to define the vision for service excellence in the library. That vision needs to be so strong and motivating that it activates and moves employees and the library toward excellence. How do you begin to develop a powerful vision of service excellence? You start imagining the perfect library environment from the customer's and employee's perspectives. What would the ideal workplace be like? What surroundings would you like as an employee? How about customers? Can you imagine what kind of environment and services your customers want? Customers come in many segments, so imagine this environment from a student's perspective, from the perspective of a child, or from that of a faculty member.

   The next step is to work with members of the management team to communicate the vision of service excellence. Develop a philosophy and value statement that illuminates your library's vision.

   The Lockton Insurance Agency has stated it's mission, commitment and philosophies in these statements. The statements are printed on small business cards for employees throughout the organization as well as framed and hung in many locations.

   The library director is bigger than life to the employees. The director's behaviors are watched and talked about. Directors set the expectations, tone, vision, and culture of the library. They set the rules and establish the systems.

   Like Jan Carlson at SAS, the library director who must shape the middle management behavior so that these managers internalize higher standards and demonstrate behavior that sets and supports the example for the entire workforce.

   As you will recall, it was Jan Carlson's strategy to transform SAS into an obsession with customer needs and desires. After an initial tremendous success, the standards at Scandinavian Airlines started to slide again. Planes started being late, employees were less cheerful, and service in general seemed to be getting sloppy. As they analyzed the difficulty, management concluded that the quick change, with its emphasis on the customer, had bypassed the middle managers. Front-line people got attention, rewards and recognition, and more authority to solve problems. Because the managers felt left out, they resisted the changes. They continued to operate as in the past, defending their turf.

FIGURE 4-1: The Lockton Insurance Agency

THE LOCKTON MISSION:

To be the worldwide value and service leader in insurance brokerage and risk management services.

THE LOCKTON COMMITMENT:

To provide the most uncommon results and service in a most common business.

THE LOCKTON PHILOSOPHIES:

The Lockton Insurance Agency will:

- Be committed to the highest standards of excellence in everything we do.
- Practice the Golden Rule and sustain a highly ethical, moral, and caring culture.
- Recognize our Associates as our most valuable asset.
- Provide opportunity and support to allow all Associates to grow, improve, and achieve their ultimate potential.
- Recognize and substantially reward exemplary Associate performance.
- Respect, value, and nurture each of our client and carrier relationships.
- Be composed of people who demonstrate a passion for delivering unparalleled service internally and externally.
- Make a recognizable difference to our clients' business through innovative solutions to their insurance needs.
- Be proactive in sustaining a meaningful corporate social and civic responsibility.
- Maintain our independence and private ownership.
- Manage our business for consistent and orderly growth.
- Be a fiercely competitive and aggressive sales organization.
- Generate fair and healthy financial returns.

FIGURE 4-2: Your Mission, Your Service Vision, Your Philosophies

The Mission of Your Library:

Your Service Vision:

Your Philosophies:

---

2. *Practice what you preach and set the standard and the example.* Administrators can change staff's perceptions by demonstrating personal commitment. No one in the library is exempt from customer service, not even the "big wigs." This example sets the standard.

3. *Hold people accountable.* Performance evaluations, job descriptions, and reward and recognition programs work to reinforce customer service. Top managers must hold middle managers accountable. They must develop new expectations for the middle managers. Those expectations include exemplifying good customer service and providing a good role model; developing job specific expectations for their staff; holding regular meetings to discuss customer service solutions to customer situations; monitoring customer service behavior, and confront employees who do not provide the service level necessary; and developing the necessary communication channels to listen to employees cares and concerns.

If directors are really serious about achieving service excellence, new and serious expectations must be set for middle managers. Middle managers must exemplify excellent customer relations and serve as a positive role model. Some of the things that middle managers should do include:

- Develop for every employee specific expectations that lead the employee to service excellence.
- Hold regular staff meetings to keep employees informed about issues, events, and priorities.
- Discuss customer service "cases" at staff meetings. Use these events to continue to train employees on developing "informed judgement".
- Confront employees who violate customer relations expectations. Use the disciplinary process to counsel, coach, and when necessary, terminate. Do not tolerate mediocrity.
- Develop open lines of communication with employees.
- Recognize good customer service, reward-even with a pat on the back.

4. *Empower your people.* Support them. Ask, listen, act, inform, recognize and reward.

   The managers job has been changed. In the traditional management style, the organizational structure is developed from the top down. When the customer is first, this organizational structure is turned upside down. The manager's role is to empower others. It is to help the employee serve the customer. How do you empower your employees? You provide the necessary support systems, and the necessary information and communication systems. You also reinforce through reward and recognition programs.

5. *Take risks. Stick your neck out.* The turtle is pretty slow. Even so, the only way it gets anywhere is by sticking it's neck out. Libraries need to encourage the front line staff to take a risk and suggest new ideas. "Do it. Fix it. Try it." as Tom Peters says.

6. *Go for the long haul, not the quick fix.* Don't treat service excellence as a fad. In fact, don't start service excellence programs in your library until you are committed to the long haul. It seems easy to develop programs of service excellence. However, we are talking about complete changes in management style and employee expectations. These changes require training and more training. As the level of service rises, the expectations also increase.

5 THE EMPLOYEE AS A CUSTOMER

"You can buy a person's time, you can buy a person's physical presence at a given place; you can even buy a measured number of a person's skilled muscular motions per hour. But you can not buy loyalty . . . you can not buy the devotion of hearts, minds and souls. You must earn these."

—*Clarence Francis*

Enthusiastic, happy employees make customers happy. Conversely, employees who are demoralized, who feel unappreciated, will demonstrate their feelings to the customers. If library employees don't have the confidence in their library, if they don't believe in its services and feel a stake in its future, the library has a deep-seated problem that no amount of public relations or promotion can fix.

Libraries accomplish their goals through their employees. If the employees don't perform, the library does not perform.

EMPLOYEE NEEDS AND WANTS

A. H. Maslow designed a hierarchy of human needs. Maslow claimed that the basic needs for survival, including food and shelter, had to be satisfied first. These basic needs are survival needs. After these survival needs are met, the person's needs are raised to the next level. Those needs identified by Maslow are included in Figure 5-1.

Survival needs for food and shelter are met through gainful employment. Employees are often attracted to the library setting because of the inherent stability that provides a sense of safety and security in the job marketplace. Now, rapid changes in the library industry can make library employees feel tense and insecure.

The next level of needs, dealing with social needs, has to do with belonging and group identification. When employees feel included in decision making processes, these needs are met. However, when employees feel isolated from management, these social needs of identification are threatened.

Ego needs include the need for appreciation, and respect in the eyes of others. A simple pat on the back or recognition of

FIGURE 5-1: Maslow's Heirarchy of Needs

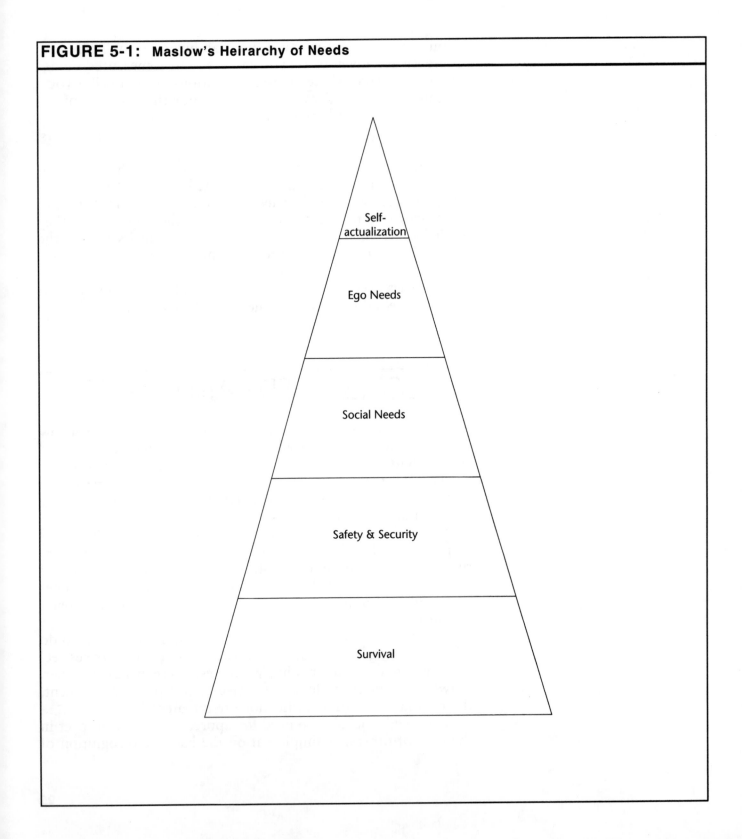

individual accomplishments goes a long way toward meeting these needs.

The final level of need for self-actualization emerges when the other needs are largely satisfied. Here the needs are for job enrichment, opportunity, growth and education, creativity, the opportunity to take on a challenge, risk and innovation and employee involvement in solving difficult library organization problems.

If the library can meet the self-actualization needs of the employees, the library or employer benefits because the employee is productive, motivated, enthusiastic, and fulfilled. This employee can provide the best customer service to fellow employees and to customers. It is important to remember that all employees have the needs that Maslow describes. Ego needs and the needs for self actualization occur at every level within the organization and not just with the administrators.

In order to develop superior service, the library must have motivated employees who will go that extra step for customers. Employees want good working conditions, good bosses, communication, respect, participation, recognition of achievement, advancement, as well as compensation and job security. Compensation is usually not the most important item in this list.

In terms of supervision, employees want managers who are supportive, who keep them informed about policy decisions and who consult them on decisions that affect their jobs. They want to know the total picture and how they fit in to that picture. They want a clear definition of the expectations. They also want to know the specific criteria by which their performance will be judged—for example, the level of service, courtesy, quality, quantity, innovation, and self-development. They want performance standards in both quantitative and qualitative terms. They want periodic progress reviews to let them know how they are doing and where they stand.

Let's look at some of these employee desires more closely.

Working conditions. Only a few libraries have enough room. Often employees are placed in crowded and uncomfortable working conditions. While you can't have offices like those in private industry, the offices can be clean. There is a need for privacy, for clean restrooms and lounges. Fixtures and furniture should be maintained in proper order and not allowed to drift into a state of despair.

Compensation. It is important that compensation be competitive with other organizations outside the library. It is also important that the compensation be equitable internally.

Employees measure their self worth in terms of what they earn. Further, employees who feel that they are improperly compensated in relation to one another or to comparable jobs within the library will feel cheated. In these situations, morale is usually quite poor. And it is the customer who suffers.

Achievement. The majority of people who come to work want to do the best job that they can. Each one has a built in "need to achieve," and a need to be recognized for that achievement. If people are deprived of the opportunity to achieve, they adapt an "I don't care" attitude.

Public recognition for achievement sets a tone for the entire library. The individual so recognized grows ten feet tall. It stimulates others to grow and to achieve too.

Monetary awards for achievement are not the only awards. You can give provide recognition, a pat on the back, free lunches, free parking places, praise, and the opportunity to achieve again.

Employee Involvement. People feel good about themselves when they are totally immersed in the library. Performance teams and participatory management make them feel important. They develop a sense of ownership and stewardship. The customer, of course, benefits.

People also make the best decisions when they make those decisions through the collective wisdom of the group. Participation reduces the resistance to change and gives employees a sense of ownership.

HOW DO YOU KNOW IF YOU ARE MEETING YOUR EMPLOYEES NEEDS?

There are market research tools you can use to provide you with the insight you needs.

Focus Groups

One way of assessing your employees needs is through focus groups (see chapter 9 on market research). Randomly select groups of employees (12-18 in each group). A facilitator from outside the work environment will create an appropriate environment for employees to express their honest opinions. The discussion guide should include questions concerning the following: The employees economic well being, safety, and security (working conditions, compensation, benefits), belonging (social interaction, group opportunities, participation in the decision making process, organization traditions that build a sense of identification), ego (reward and recognition programs, praise, promotions, pats on the back), and self-actualization (the chance to do something that matters, personal enthusiasms.)

Employee Audit

Provide every employee with a simple audit on the issues covered above. Employees should fill the documents out and return them to a designated location. There should be no signatures. Employee responses may surprise you. Their answers may be different from what you expected. The information provided through this simple audit is simply directional information only. This survey will act like a camera in that it will provide a picture of the problem areas. You will have to do additional research to fully understand the problems.

Figure 5.2 is a sample questionnaire. You should add questions that personalize this survey to your library.

Employee Surveys

Many organizations and corporations do an annual survey of their employees. These surveys done on an annual basis provide an ongoing barometer of employee issues. Employees do not sign their names to their survey response. Questionnaires are usually mailed to an outside research firm or organization. Results are tabulated and analyzed by a group of employees, not individuals.

CASE STUDY

SALT LAKE CITY PUBLIC LIBRARY

Administrators of libraries often feel that they are limited in terms of their ability to provide growth opportunities to meet staff needs. Employees of libraries tend to remain with the organization for many years. There is little turnover and limited promotional opportunity. How do you meet the self-actualization needs of employees in this kind of environment. The Salt Lake City Public Library responded in the following way to such a challenge.

FIGURE 5-2: Sample test or employee audit. The more yes answers, the better. "No" answers indicate areas that need improvement.

How does the library rate with employees?

Directions: Circle the appropriate answer.

1. Employees feel appreciated by management   yes   no

2. Does the management team act on the belief that if they can make employees happy, the employees will make customers happy?   yes   no

3. Does the library have special events or gestures of appreciation at least monthly?   yes   no

4. Do employees feel respected by the library director and management team?   yes   no

5. Does the library have rituals or traditions that build a sense of community and a sense of belonging for employees?   yes   no

6. Does the management team encourage employee involvement and participation in problem solving?   yes   no

7. Does the library celebrate employee length of service?   yes   no

8. Are retirees recognized?   yes   no

9. Do you have spontaneous events periodically just to boost employee morale?   yes   no

In 1990, the Salt Lake City Public Library reorganized as an outcome of a staff utilization evaluation. The staff had identified that there were major problems within the organization. Burnout, stress, boredom, career stagnation, lack of turnover, and poor job/people match were all major problems. The administration proposed the following to stimulate renewed opportunity for learning skills:

- All interested staff should send their name and any position(s) in which they were interested to the personnel office in writing. A list of open positions was sent to staff members who indicated an interest in any position. The personnel staff did not know, nor could they determine what positions might come open when the shifts started to occur.

- Many lateral changes did occur in the system as a result. Lateral moves did not effect pay, seniority or eligibility for merit raises. Reclassification within a current position was not included in the process.

- Flexibility in the job descriptions and hours for some part-time positions took place. Hours were exchanged by adding to some positions or combining two part-time jobs for one full-time position.

How successful was the program? Staff who moved to new departments were overwhelmingly successful. Staff learned flexibility, and exhibited a willingness to pitch-in unfamiliar departments. The excitement has renewed employee enthusiasm. The library has seen a break in the old Main vs. the Branches mentality that they, like so many systems, had suffered under. New friendships and new teams were developed with co-workers unknown to each other in the past. For the staff who participated, there were expanded resumes, skills, and creative ideas in professional development.

FIGURE 5-3: Employee Survey—How does the library rate?

1. How would you rate the library in general as compared with other employers.

    1. About the best

    2. Much better than most

    3. The same as others

    4. Not as good as others

2. How satisfied are you with your job or the kind of work you do?

    1. Very satisfied

    2. Somewhat satisfied

    3. Neither satisfied nor dissatisfied

    4. Somewhat dissatisfied

    5. Very dissatisfied

(continued)

FIGURE 5-3: (Cont.)

3. I consider my future opportunities at the library to be:

1. Excellent

2. Good

3. Fair

4. Poor

5. Not concerned about future advancement

Please provide your comments

_____

_____

4. How do you feel about the present rate of pay compared with rates paid for other libraries?

1. Higher

2. About the same

3. Lower

5. How well do you feel you are informed about the library and your department activities. (circle one answer for each item)

	The Library	Your Department
Well informed	1	1
Usually informed	2	2
Seldom informed	3	3
Poorly informed	4	4

6. How would you rate the library on the following benefits? Please circle one answer for each item.

	Excellent	Good	Fair	Poor
Insurance programs				
Health Insurance	1	2	3	4
Dental Insurance	1	2	3	4
Vision Care	1	2	3	4
lcohol/drug rehabilitation	1	2	3	4

(continued)

FIGURE 5-3: (Cont.)

	Excellent	Good	Fair	Poor
Retirement program				
Pension plan	1	2	3	4
Early retirement program	1	2	3	4
Time off with pay	1		2	34
Number of paid holidays	1	2	3	4
Sick days	1	2	3	4
Vacation with pay	1	2	3	4
Overall benefits	1	2	3	4

Comments:

_____

_____

7. How do you rate the following employee services? (Please circle one answer for each item)

	Excellent	Good	Fair	Poor
Employee parking	1	2	3	4
Employee counseling	1	2	3	4
Service award program	1	2	3	4
Handling of grievances	1	2	3	4
Recognition of you as an individual	1	2	3	4
Administration of suggestion plan	1	2	3	4
Tuition refund program	1	2	3	4

Comments:

_____

_____

(continued)

FIGURE 5-3: (Cont.)

8. The following have been added or changed. What are your opinions of each? (Please circle one answer for each item.)

Smoking policy	1	2	3	4
Employee party	1	2	3	4

Comments:

_____

_____

9. What other programs do you think should be added or improved upon?

_____

_____

10. What do you think of your immediate supervisor's behavior on these areas? (Please circle one answer for each item)

Being helpful when you have a question or suggestion regarding work	1	2	3	4
Showing you how to do your work better	1	2	3	4
Being fair to everyone	1	2	3	4
Giving recognition	1	2	3	4
Communicating	1	2	3	4
Explaining library policies	1	2	3	4
Evaluating performance	1	2	3	4
Promoting teamwork	1	2	3	4
Resolving problems	1	2	3	4
Overall performance of your immediate supervisor	1	2	3	4

SATISFYING THE EMPLOYEE CUSTOMER

There are many methods for satisfying employee customers. Here are just a few:

- Establish an employee affairs committee. This committee can serve to take the pulse of the organization, take a look at issues that affect employees, as well as participate in the development of events.

- Communication. Develop in-house newsletters, announcements, memos and informal communication programs that keep employees informed. These communication channels should be two-way, up as well as down.

- Develop participation opportunities. Teams, quality circles, and task forces offer employees opportunities to be involved in problem solving and decision making.

BUILDING THE CUSTOMER ORIENTED WORK FORCE

HIRING THE RIGHT PEOPLE

When interviewing individuals for a job within a library, the library's values need to be clearly emphasized. The importance of customer service has to be made clear. Open ended questions should be asked by the interviewer. Interviewees should be asked to solve real or hypothetical customer service situations.

The best way to select those with a customer-service orientation and to screen out those who are deficient in this area is through the interviewing process. The goal of the interview is to select those individuals who have, in their life and work experience, demonstrated a service orientation. Some of the behavioral characteristics that make up a service orientation include good oral communication skills, cooperation and teamwork, problem solving and decision making skills, enthusiasm, high energy level, and flexibility and adaptability.

In the interview process, you need to look beyond the technical competence. Determine "people skills". Ask interview questions which provide an opportunity to understand if the candidate has the right approach to customer service.

ORIENTATION—STARTING OUT ON THE RIGHT FOOT

An orientation program may well mean the difference between success and failure for a new employee. As was stated earlier in the examples of superstar organizations, all of them have an intense employee orientation process, both in the classroom and on the job. An employee who feels important and welcome will make customers feel important and welcome.

The orientation process should include the following:

1. Presentations by top administrators, including a message describing the importance of customer service for both internal and external customers.

2. Tours of the library and services with introductions to service personnel.

3. Customer service training sessions. These sessions should include an introduction to customer service, sample problems for group solving, videos and demonstrations, as well as any guidebook used by the library. If appropriate, the training should include sessions on how to handle an angry customer, telephone training and library systems training.

4. Set clear expectations to new employees about what constitutes excellent job performance. Identify customer service issues as a part of performance evaluation. Explain performance standards and evaluation process.

5. Encourage opportunities for people to mix with each other and develop a bond between them. Explain the values, traditions, customers, and reward system of the library.

Two months after the orientation process, reconvene the new employees for breakfast to find out about their first two months on the job. Have them provide an evaluation of their orientation process. What else did they need to know?

JOB DESCRIPTIONS SET THE STANDARD

Often employees do not understand exactly what they are responsible for and accountable for. Although it is easy to assume that an employee knows exactly what to do and how to do it, it should be written down or it will not happen.

At McDonald's, everybody has a written job description. This job description serves as a tool for establishing performance standards, setting goals, coaching performance, and conducting appraisal reviews. These job descriptions incorporate the organizations objectives for quality, service, cleanliness, and value to the customer.

To every job description add an additional paragraph about your expectations in customer service. Such a paragraph might read: "Works with customers, either internal or external. Exhibits excellent customer relationships with customers, fellow employees. Shows courtesy, compassion and respect."

PERFORMANCE STANDARDS—A CONSTANT REMINDER

It is difficult to establish excellence until measurable and obtainable standards are put into place. Employees need to have a target to aim for.

Performance standards are difficult to establish in any organization, but particularly in libraries. Are there standards about how many books can be shelved? The work a clerical person does? The first attempt at establishing standards is usually imperfect. Standards need to be reviewed on a regular basis and revised as appropriate.

The Salt Lake City Public Library maintains a performance appraisal system for staff to document performance, plan for individual growth and professional development, and to provide a consistent basis for productivity and employee evaluation. The system exists to provide a format for staff to map out a plan for excellence and achievement on the job and within their own professional careers. The system also provides an evaluation framework for supervisors to make recommendations on salary increases and to identify needed improvements. The system is reviewed on a three year cycle.

The Performance Appraisal System has two major components. Systemwide Minimum Performance Standards have been developed over a number of years and have been reviewed by the entire staff. Newer items include suggestions by staff to ensure a more consistent form of evaluation. These principles define the performance expectations of each City Library staff member. Included in the Systemwide Minimum Performance Standards for supervisors are an additional responsibility statement for supervisors and the Mission Statement.

The second part of the performance appraisal system process is individual goal and objective setting. It is not meant to be a restatement of the position description. Goals and objectives are developed in support of annual departmental and systemwide goals and areas of individually defined growth and development. Each staff member is responsible for the development of their own goals, the objectives identified to obtain them, and to accomplish the specific actions that will be used to achieve success. The following values may need discussion and negotiation between employee and supervisor, and are expected to be integrated into employees goals.

- Quality of Work—Expected accuracy levels and how to measure them.

- Quantity of Work—Amount of acceptable work to be done.

- Use of Judgement—When and how sound decisions are to be made; what appropriate action may be taken in identified situations.

Goals, objectives, and actions are negotiated with supervisors so that they may be melded with those of the department. Additionally other performance standards in certain specific areas, such as reference, may be appended to performance appraisals. Some departments have developed specific departmental minimum standards, and these too are part of the document for those staffers.

Training is available to staff and managers on an annual basis to ensure best use oft he management of the Performance Appraisal System. Training will specifically include negotiation, communication skills, and consistency in evaluation. The orientation process covers performance planning for new staff.

All employees are part of the Performance Appraisal System process, but not all are eligible to receive merit increases during any given year. All employees, regardless of when they were hired, whose salaries do not exceed the standard range, receive wage adjustments at appropriate times. New employees formally negotiated their performance plan by the third month in a new position, and they must have worked in the performance plan system for a minimum of nine months before they qualify for a merit increase.

Recommendations for merits may be made to the Administration at the following levels:

- 0 percent—staff member is not meeting standards of position (represents 5 percent of employees).

- 2.5 percent—Staff member is meeting all standards of position and is working appropriately at job level (40 percent).

- 5 percent—Staff member shows pattern of performance which can be demonstrated to frequently exceed negotiated standards (50 percent).

- 7.5 percent—Staff member exhibits outstanding performance, ranking in the top 10 percent of the system's work force (10 percent).

EMPLOYEE COMMUNICATION

"Nobody ever tells me anything." "Who cares. They think we're nobodies." "Why do we see it in the newspapers first?" These laments are often heard from employees because of inadequate communication from administration, department heads, governing boards, from anyone perceived to have power and monopoly in information. Employees feel alienated and resentful if they are not "let in" on the library's objectives, challenges and issues. If it is truly their library, they must be kept informed.

Good communication builds commitment, investment, ownership. It gives people the opportunity to feel informed. It shows respect for employees. There are a lot of fallacies about information:

1. Assuming middle managers are an effective information funnel.

2. Thinking that a problem must be solved before it is news.

3. Thinking that no news means no need to communicate.

Employees want to know the following:

1. Where the library is going.

2. What vision the leaders have.

3. What values drive the leaders.

4. How the library is doing.

5. What the problems are and their consequences.

The employees want to feel that:

FIGURE 5-4: Memo to Staff

CONGRATULATIONS!

Circulation is up!
Every branch reported an increase in circulation this month!

Not only that . . . library
card registration increased by ten percent!

Customer surveys indicate that the library is providing excellent service.

You're making it happen! Thanks

1. This is their organization too.
2. That everyone is in it together.
3. That administrators hear and listen to employees and that they care, respect, rely on and appreciate employees.

To achieve these needs, consider the following steps:

- Vehicles for communication.
- Publish a staff update on a regular basis.

- If your library is going through a construction process, put out a facilities update.

- Set up breakfast informal sessions or brown-bag lunches.

- Put bulletin boards in staff areas.

- Publish reports from administrators.

In summary, remember that customer relations mirror employee relations. Employees will treat the customers as they are treated within the organization. Employees who like the library and feel like an important team members will be helpful and enthusiastic with customers.

6 STAFF TRAINING

Train, train, and retrain. When you first implement a customer service program, there is a significant need for training. Training should continue for all staff throughout the years. Customers' expectations will continue to rise. New technology and programs will continue to enhance the personal and professional growth of employees.

There are several different types of training that are required to implement a good customer service program

1. New employee orientation. Included within the new employee orientation should be training sessions on using the telephone, or how to deal with an angry customer.

2. Sessions for staff in general including "How to diffuse conflict" "informed judgement." There are no right answers to "informed judgement." The only way staff develop the skills is through continual training examples, and personal effort.

3. Training for managers and supervisors. This training should include programs on team building, individuals, and delegating. The training should also include how to use case examples within staff meetings.

Developing staff skills in using informed judgement comes slowly. Staffers are afraid to take risks. They want to use rules and procedures as a safety net. Employees have to learn to think of a customer's interest first as they make decisions. Staffers learn through discussion of case studies at staff meetings.

Here are four case examples to discuss in your staff meeting. Watch customers within your library setting. You will gather more and more case studies to discuss at staff meetings. This constant reinforcement and group guidance will assist the staff in developing a consistent "informed judgement."

GROUP DISCUSSIONS

A child, aged 10, comes to the desk to check out some books. His mother is standing behind him with an unpleasant look on

---

FIGURE 6-1: **Sample Questions for Staff Training Informed Judgment**

1. A customer has received an over-due notice for a book that she believes she has returned to the library? What steps would you take to work with this customer?

2. You have been away from the library for two days. There are a number of pink slips indicating phone calls you should return. Do you return calls to customers from outside the library before you return those of fellow employees? Explain

3. A vendor has submitted a bill for payment. How long do you believe it should take for the library to pay that bill? Why?

4. You are at the reference desk. A customer has requested that you give him some instructions on using the automated catalogue. There is a line behind him. The phone rings at the same time. How do you provide good customer service to all of these customers?

---

her face. The young man does not have his card with him. You look it up on the computer to find that he has had ten different cards registered to him recently. He is also blocked from checking out more material because he has not returned other books.

How would you provide handle this situation? Remember, you want to encourage the child to become a "good customer."

1. A college-age customer comes to you for help. He does not have any money, needs to copy material, and each page costs 10 cents. What do you do?

2. The college age customer has now learned that if he looks for you, you will provide free copies. Now what do you do?

3. A customer comes to the library and wants to check out material. However, she does not have a library card and no proof of identification with her. What do you do?

4. A student arrives at your desk and desperately needs to take home a reference book for a term paper due in the morning. He promises to have the book back at 8 a.m. You allow the reference book to be taken out of the library and it does not come back at 8 a.m. The student brings it in at 4:30 in the afternoon. What do you do?

TELEPHONE TRAINING

Some of the basic training for staff involves training on the telephone. When you are communicating face to face, your message is conveyed in three different ways, as follows:

1. Through your words
2. Through your voice
3. Through your body language

On the telephone, only your voice and your words are used in communication. The importance of body language is diminished. Your words and your tone of voice take on special significance. You are communicating everything through what you say and how you say it. When you answer the phone, state the name of the library, your department and your name. "Blueberry Hill Public Library, Humanities Department. This is Sam Jones. How may I help you?"

FIGURE 6-2: Telephone Training

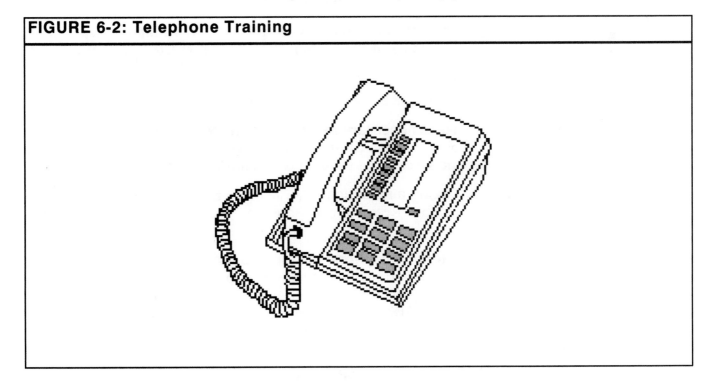

Practical telephone etiquette: Be courteous. Say "Please" and "Thank you." Use business-like phrases instead of slang.

Say "yes" instead of "yeah." Personalize your conversation by using the caller's name. Listen attentively. Take notes while the caller is speaking. Verify the information the caller gives you. Acknowledge that you hear the caller. Speak clearly, using a low pitched voice. Avoid using library jargon. Avoid talking with anything in your mouth such as gum or candy. Avoid giving out personal information about staff (addresses and phone numbers.)

Handling calls: Answer the phone promptly, ideally by the third ring. Give the caller your full attention. Don't be in the process of holding a conversation with someone else when you pick up the phone. Smile. A smile reflects warmth in your voice.

Putting callers on hold: Ask permission. Explain why and for how long. Be prepared for a caller who does not wish to be put on hold. Try to assist her/him immediately or take the caller's name and phone number and indicate you or someone else will call back. When a caller gives permission to be put on hold, return within two minutes. If you are unable to meet the caller's request within two minutes, offer to call back.

Transferring a call: Give the caller the number, department, and name of the person that you are transferring the call to. If the line is busy when you transfer the caller, ask the customer if he or she would like to call the number directly and repeat the number and the department and/or name.

Tools necessary for good telephone communication: Paper, pens and pencils for note-taking, message pads for recording messages and a list of phone numbers of other departments.

Taking a message: Write down the date and time, and phone number. Record the message, sign your name, and deliver the message.

Internal telephone customer service: Respect your co-worker's time by stating the purpose of your call immediately. Show patience when a co-worker calls and interrupts your own work. Always ask if it is convenient for that person to take your call. Take the time to acknowledge good telephone service when you receive it.

Handling the irate caller: Don't let the caller's anger control your attitude! Listen, acknowledge the situation, agree and apologize, offer concern (don't take the comments personally), take action ("I'm sorry that you are upset. What can I do to help you?"). End the call or refer it to your supervisor.

DELIVERING EXCELLENT SERVICE FOR YOUR CUSTOMERS

A few hints for personal interaction: Good customer service depends on these factors: reliability; the ability to provide the information, assistance, answer the questions, provide the special events and programs that were promised; responsiveness; the willingness of every employee to help the customer promptly; assurance; the knowledge and courtesy you show to customers, and your ability to convey trust, competence, and confidence; empathy; the degree of caring and individual attention you show customers. It also depends on tangibles; the provision of facilities, books and information , materials, equipment, and your own (and others') appearance.

For customers visiting your library
Wear identification badges. They help identify you as an employee and a person who can be of assistance. Know where your customers can find amenities (restrooms and water fountains) and auxiliary services. Where can customers get Friends' membership information, information about special events. Know what special events or programs are going on.

Smile. If a customer looks confused, ask if you can help. If you can not answer a customer's question, take him or her to an individual who can help. Remember that the secret of success depends on three things: words, voice, and body language. Communication is not just with words. The tone of your voice and your body language make a huge difference in the response received from the customer. You indicate whether or not you are approachable through body language. Acknowledge your customer as an individual through eye contact. Listen carefully to the customer. Often a customer just wants someone to listen to his or her complaint or need. Avoid tightly closed arms, tucking your hands into pockets, or clenching your fists. Convey confidence through good posture . . . and smile.

7 PROBLEM SOLVING AND COMPLAINT MANAGEMENT

"Complaints give us an opportunity to hear from our customers. They give us an opportunity to improve our service."

Problems and complaints are inevitable. How can we use those problems and complaints to listen to our customers? As a tool to improve our services? Obviously, we need to develop a system to hear those complaints. We need to make it easy for our customers to talk to us, to express their concerns, complaints, and complements, too. We need to develop a system that ensures responsiveness by the entire library system and not just one office.

Problems interfere with customer satisfaction. In fact, they are the most direct form of feedback we have from customers. If something doesn't go right, the customer wants it fixed right now! Problems also affect employee morale. If employees see a problem that they can't do anything about, it takes value away from their job.

Complaints come in several forms. Sometimes they are in person, in a confrontation. Other times, they arrive through the mail in writing. Either way, there are some simple guidelines to use in responding to them, as follows:

1. Respond immediately. Customers need to feel that someone is listening now! Often the fact that you are listening and trying to resolve the issue is more important than the solution. Even if the complaint comes through the mail, a quick turnaround is important to the customer.

2. Stress what you can do for the customer, not what you can't do . If you can't let the customer take out ten books because of restrictions on the card, stress that he or she can check out two or three until you get the issue resolved.

3. Don't challenge the customer. Don't try to win an argument. You will only make him or her more angry. Stay calm and keep the conversation in a neutral area. Concentrate on trying to find a solution that you both can live with.

4. Allow the customer to express his anger. Don't take the anger personally. Keep calm and let it blow over your head. After the customer vents his or her anger, he or she can calm down enough to agree on a solution.

5. If rules or procedures are the issue, state them in such a way that they benefit the customer.

Problems occur with internal customers as well as external customers. Issues arise between different departments. Again, we need to treat internal customers as we would external customers. We need to listen and strive to develop solutions.

DEVELOPING A CUSTOMER FEEDBACK SYSTEM

We need to hear from our customers on an ongoing basis. To do that, we need to develop customer feedback systems. There are informal as well as informal systems that are easily put into place. They include focus groups, community forums, as well as simple luncheon meetings with a group of customers. for example, invite a group of customers in once a month for a simple lunch. Ask them for their input about library services. What do they like? Where do they perceive you could provide better service?

How about written complaints? The Denver Public Library has developed a system to encourage customer feedback, in the terms of complaints and complements. It has developed a printed card that is displayed on all circulation, reference, and department desks. Customers with either a problem, complaint or salutation are encouraged by the library staff to fill in a card and mail it (postage paid) back to the Assistant to the City Librarian.

Again, a quick response is the key. When a card arrives at the office of the Assistant to the City Librarian, it is dealt with immediately. If the issue is a systemwide concern, the Assistant to the City Librarian answers the customer complaint immediately himself. If the complaint, salutation, or problem deals with a specific person, department or branch library, the information is sent to the manager in the area. The manager responds within five days. A copy of the response is sent back to the Assistant to the City Librarian. The response is attached to the card and put in a finished file.

When asked about what kinds of complaints or salutations they receive, the Assistant to the City Librarian indicated that 90 percent of the cards commenting on staff cite the excellent

FIGURE 7-1: Denver Public Library Customer Suggestions

AGENCY _____

Dear Denver Public Library Customer:

How are we doing? Meeting your needs is our most important goal. Your concerns and comments mean a lot to us. If we're not meeting your needs, please let us know. If we are doing our job well, we'd like to hear that also. Thank you for sharing your ideas and suggestions with us.

Rick J. Ashton

Rick Ashton, City Librarian

Dear Rick:

Date _____

_____

Name _____

Address _____

_____

Zip _____   Phone _____

Denver Public Library

9/91/15M

FIGURE 7-2: Denver Public Library Customer Suggestions

Were you treated courteously? _____
_____
_____

Did you find what you needed? _____
_____
_____

What else would you like to tell us? _____
_____
_____

||||

No
Postage Stamp
Necessary
if Mailed in the
United States

BUSINESS REPLY MAIL
FIRST CLASS MAIL   PERMIT NO. 2062   DENVER, CO

POSTAGE WILL BE PAID BY:

DENVER PUBLIC LIBRARY

1357 Broadway
Denver, CO 80203-9849

service that individual staff members have provided. Customers also use the cards to make collection selection recommendations. The library is very responsive to customer suggestions regarding collection materials. The remainder of the cards concern service issues. Service issues include such issues as a broken bookmobile, and whether the building is too hot or too cold.

Every time a change is made within the library system, the Assistant to the City Librarian sees an increase in the number of cards. Library closings or openings, rehabilitation, construction, personnel changes, and relocations of collection material always encourage customers to let the library know how they feel.

The customer cards are also very useful for the library in personnel evaluations. the behavior of staff members who continually receive accolades for exemplary service is reinforced through positive evaluations. Conversely, those employees who demonstrate poor customer service, and whose poor service is documented through customer input, feel the impact on their evaluation.

Records of complaints should be kept. A checksheet enables you to tabulate and to track the frequency of complaints. This will enable you to understand the urgency with which complaints should be dealt with.

How do you decide which complaints or problems need to be addressed? How do you determine the priority? One solution is to develop a Pareto chart to determine which problems or complaints to address. Pareto was an Italian economist (1848-1882) who conducted a study of the wealth in Europe. He found that 80 percent of the wealth was in the hands of 20 percent of the population. Sounds familiar, doesn't it? It is the old 80/20 rule. Companies find that 80 percent of their business comes from 20 percent of their customers. Probably 80 percent of the circulation comes from 20 percent of the library customers. Eighty percent of the donations to a campaign come from 20 percent of the donors. In the same way, 80 percent of the employee issues come from 20 percent of the employees.

By developing a Pareto chart, we can prioritize the top 80 percent of the complaints or problems that need to be addressed.

FIGURE 7-3: **A check sheet for complaints**

Customer complaints		number
Rude library staff member	xxxxxxxxxxxxxx	14
return date not clearly marked	xxxxxxxxxxx	11
evening hours too short	xx	2
waited too long for service	xxxxxxxxxxxxxxxxx	17
Poor selection of materials	xxx	3
library space too cramped	xxxx	4
overdue fines too expensive	xxxxxx	6
Poor location	x	1
Materials poorly displayed	xxx	3
Not enough variation in materials	xxxx	4
poorly lit	xxxxxxx	7
no place to sit	xxx	3

Total   75

FIGURE 7-4: **Calculate the Percentages**

1.	17	22.67%
2.	14	18.67%
3.	11	14.67%
4.	7	9.33%
5.	6	8%
6.	4	5.33%
7.	4	5.33%
8.	3	4%
9.	3	4%
10.	3	4%
11.	2	2.67%
12.	1	1.33%

1. Obtain the data. Develop a check sheet.

2. Review the data. Identify the most frequent problems. Place them in order down to the least frequent.

FIGURE 7-5: Pareto Diagram

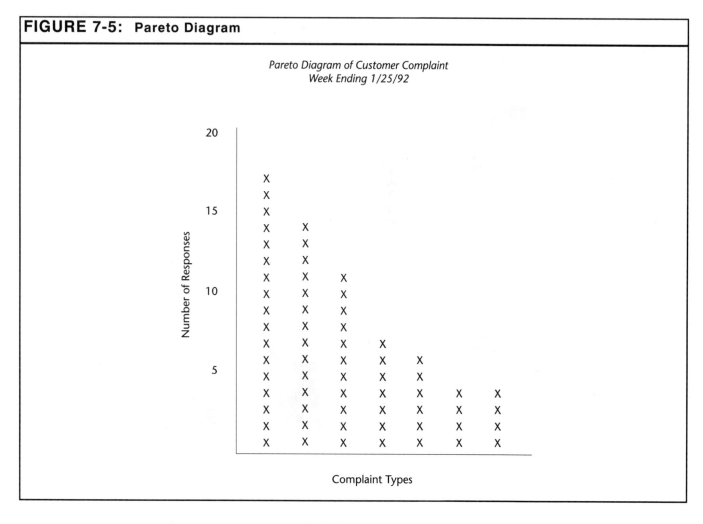

Pareto Diagram of Customer Complaint
Week Ending 1/25/92

Complaint Types

3. Calculate the percentages.

4. Determine the vital few from the important many. The Pareto chart assists us in identifying which problem to be attacked. We want to look for 80 percent of the problems or opportunities to solve.

5. Develop a diagram. Develop a bar for each of the categories of problems on a diagram in descending order from left to right

6. Determine which problems to attack as well as the priority order. Identify the top 80 percent through the Pareto chart.

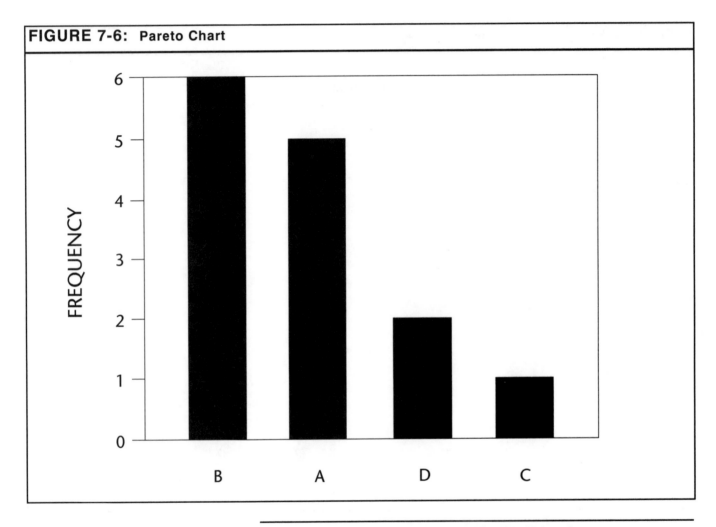

FIGURE 7-6: Pareto Chart

SOLVING THE PROBLEMS

Create a team, task force/special unit. This is one of the best ways of empowering individuals, helping them to feel a part of the organization as well as solving the problems. These teams should included members at different levels within the organization who are affected by the problem.

The development of fully functioning teams is not an easy matter. Teams need guidance and guidelines. They need assistance to develop the communication skills, openness, trust, and mutual support. Staff members appointed to special teams or task forces have an opportunity to develop and demonstrate leadership skills and problem solving skills. A good team doesn't just happen. At first, the individuals grouped together

FIGURE 7-7: Prioritizing problems to be solved

1. Waited too long for service	17	22.67%
2. Rude library staff member	14	18.67%
3. Return date not clearly marked	11	14.67%
4. Poorly lit	7	9.33%
5. Overdue fines too expensive	6	8%
6. Library space too cramped	4	5.33%
7. Not enough variation in materials	4	5.33%
Total		84%

Total	75	100%

are unclear about the group's purpose. They recommend decisions without considering the group purpose. An outside administrator should work with the team to clarify its purpose, to keep meetings focused and to assist the team in gathering momentum. Overtime, as members of the group will begin to respect and trust other members of the team, but they may not yet have a strong commitment to the team. Again, outside assistance can assist the team in coming together. Eventually the members of the team will feel personally committed to fulfilling the purpose. Their purpose will be clear, and their achievements will be remarkable.

In order to achieve this level, trust between team members has to be established. Controlling behavior, manipulation, indifference, superiority and judging will be destructive to the development of a successful team. Those behaviors that need to be encouraged are openness, equality, risk taking and a focus on the problem at hand. Teams elect a chairperson as well as a secretary to take notes and schedule meetings. Team members must be allowed to have the time to participate in the meetings. Restricting the meetings to one hour in length puts a minimum of scheduling problems on staff. The team spends the first meeting in clarifying the purpose of its assignment and determining the length of time they perceive it will take to develop a solution.

This type of team approach to problem solving requires that administrators trust and empower individuals of the staff at all levels within the organization. Participation and idea generation should be encouraged of all of the members of the team. Creating and encouraging the development of effective teams requires the following:

1. Changing roles for managers again.

2. Developing shared responsibility by team members and administrators.

3. Developing a shared vision.

4. Building trust and communication among team members.

5. Eliminating manipulation, judging, and other behaviors that stop communication.

6. Stimulating creative solutions.

CREATIVE THINKING/BRAINSTORMING

Creative thinking is fun for employees. There are some rules to encourage creative thinking, as follows:

1. That there are no bad ideas.

2. Crazy ideas are encouraged (they encourage others to think beyond the typical paradigms of the organization).

3. It is OK to take a risk.

4. Every idea is a good one.

5. Don't stop too soon.

Try your hand at creative thinking! List as many ideas as you can think of to improve your current job in the next two minutes.

1. _____

2. _____

3. _____

4. _____

5. _____

6. _____

7. _____

8. _____

9. _____

10. _____

11. _____

12. _____

13. _____

14. _____

15. _____

16. _____

17. _____

18. _____

19. _____

20. _____

8 REWARD AND RECOGNITION: THE KEY TO EMPLOYEE MOTIVATION

After you have launched your customer relations strategies and identified the behaviors that demonstrate excellence, you should initiate reward and recognition programs. Make sure that you design recognition programs so that they influence many people, not just a few. Design a rich variety of rewards.

A good recognition program rewards specific behavior. Your systems should recognize these behaviors, not general global goodness. Give some awards for individual, heroic acts; others for consistent, day-in day-out behavior; and some team awards or departmental awards that exemplify the internal or external customer service behavior you want to encourage.

WHY HAVE REWARD AND RECOGNITION PROGRAMS?

- Rewards Improve Everyone's Performance.

- "You cannot be a high-performing company if everybody gets a 'C.'"

- Rewards raise the level of performance. They elevate employee's awareness of what should be done.

- Recognition of both outstanding and unacceptable behavior is more motivating than benign neglect can ever be.

- Rewards for customer service set the standard for new directions.

- Tie Reward and Recognition Programs to Defined Goals and Objectives.

- "Give your employees clear, achievable goals and they will exceed them."

Your reward system works in a goal-setting environment because:

1. Rewards clarify responsibility and accountability.

2. More effort is directed to accomplishment. People stay focused.

3. People have a concrete reason for working harder.

4. Rewards promote originality and creativity.

5. Rewards foster better communication.

6. Employees are mobilized to find opportunities rather than protecting the status quo.

7. Rewards reinforce loyalty.

8. Rewards identify non-performers for you and for themselves.

NINE POINTS OF A GOOD REWARD SYSTEM

1. *Set clear targets.* For example, at the end of the year your library director should send a memo to all staff. The message should indicate a pride in the accomplishments of the library in the past year. The memo should say something like, "I realize that each department has individuals whose energetic and dedicated work singles them out to their co-workers. These individuals set an example for all of us. Therefore, we are establishing an employee recognition program to identify and reward such excellent work."

    The program should be spelled out to the employees. Clear goals and objectives must be articulated. Establish a minimum acceptance level and set priorities. Retain some flexibility in case of unanticipated events. Establish a timeline for accomplishing objectives.

2. *Make the rewards fit the goal.* Our workforce is rapidly changing in terms of age, sex, ethnic diversity, value systems, ethics, and orientation toward work. The rewards you provide may be appreciated by one group of individuals but not valued by another. For example, public recognition may be welcomed by some. But this public

recognition could be quite an embarrassment for people whose ethnic group culture supports only group efforts.

Because of financial limitations, libraries need to focus on non-monetary rewards. Those awards can include a day off, free parking, recognition events, and public displays. Make the reward fit the goal.

3. *Leverage the impact.* Provide the reward soon after the good performance. You want to strengthen the employee's association of hard work with a reward. You also want to create an environment in which other employee's recognize the hard work of their fellow employee and the reward system. If you serve coffee or hold a reception to recognize the award, give the employee a tangible certificate or plaque so that the value of the award goes far beyond one day.

4. *Celebrate the process.* When the library reaches its goals, celebrate—a picnic, a day at your local beach (or swimming hole), games in the park, or perhaps, a party at the library. Make fun of tumbles that have occurred over the past year. Encourage supervisors and administrators to have fun with the employees.

5. *Be personal.* Every individual in a supervisory role can make reward and recognition a personal matter. Take individuals on your staff out for lunch just to say thanks for a job well done. Drop a personal note to an individual when you see exemplary service. Take a moment to say thank you.

6. *Reward what really matters.* Use reward and recognition programs to reinforce the values of the library. Reward good customer service. Recognize that extra effort when you see it.

7. Include everybody. Some businesses can encourage performance through financial incentives. These financial incentives are difficult to put into place within a library. What you can do is encourage the development of team goals. Every member of the team is important to achieving those goals. Team members keep each other focused and encouraged.

8. *Shine the spotlight.* Certificates, plaques, and special recognition events shine the spotlight on exemplary service.

This spotlight reinforces the award winning efforts and encourages other employees to do likewise.

9. *Create peer pressure.* We need to do a paradigm shift to encourage good customer service. A few employees will take the lead in moving in new directions. Recognition assists in creating the peer pressure that is necessary for all of the employees to move into good service.

OTHER IDEAS

- Spotlight the exemplary people.

- Make individuals visible.

- Recognize one whole department or unit.

- Design quarterly awards.

- Develop a system to "catch good customer service."

- Get customers to report good behavior.

- Ask peers to express their appreciation.

- Reward the service oriented team.

- Reward service innovations.

IS MONEY THE ONLY REWARD?

Money is usually thought of as the only reward. However, most organizations cannot afford numerous financial awards. There are alternatives. Recognition of a job well done, opportunities for personal growth, increased control over one's job, status in the eyes of others, a better work environment—all of these alternatives demonstrate appreciation.

Imagine getting a phone call from your boss saying, "I just wanted you to know that I think you are doing a great job!" Imagine receiving a card that reads, "Bravo! Your department achieved an all-time record of service this month!"

WHICH REWARDS REWARD?

People only work harder for the things they consider valuable. That varies from person to person.

Grass-roots programs tend to be the most powerful. Be observant. Notice how people respond to different kinds of reinforcement. Rewards must be tailored to the personalities receiving them. Use trial and error and observe the results.

NON-MONETARY REWARDS

Non monetary rewards include:

- Spoken or written praise.
- A thank you and a handshake.
- An article in the library newsletter.
- Praise in the presence of the boss's boss.
- A request for or acceptance of your advice by the boss.
- The boss who drops in for chat.
- A trophy, book, or other small token of gratitude.
- Lunch or dinner with boss or peers.

BUILDING YOUR REWARD AND RECOGNITION PROGRAM

1. Start with employee involvement. Small libraries with only a few employees will find that an employee of the month program is not realistic. There are simply not enough employees. Begin with a discussion with the employees about the appropriate reward and recognition program that would be suitable.

2. In a larger library, start with an audit. What kind of formal and informal reward and recognition programs are going on at this time? Often different departments or branches have their own informal programs. How are those programs working?

3. In larger systems, focus groups with employees would be very helpful. The use of an outside facilitator allows the staff to speak honestly about current programs and provide creative ideas for the future. These focus groups will

assist you in identifying new options as well as test reactions to proposed programs.

4. Conduct a survey of your employees to see how they feel about various rewards. (Refer back to Figure 5.2, the sample survey.)

5. Develop recommended reward and recognition programs. Include both formal recognition events and informal ones. Draft a budget and identify funding sources. These reward and recognition programs can be funded by the local Friends organization, acquiring donations from local restaurants, theaters, and other places or sources.

CASE STUDIES

CASE STUDY #1—IBM CORPORATION

"I believe that if an organization is to meet the challenges of a changing world, it must be prepared to change everything about itself . . . as it moves through a corporate life."

—Thomas J. Watson, Jr.
—Former Chairman/CEO

Customer Perceptions of IBM

IBM did market research to understand how customers felt about them. These are some examples of the perceptions of customers. These perceptions influenced the direction, organization and decisions of IBM executives for the future. As we realize, IBM is still in the middle of the paradigm shift.

Customers said the following about IBM:

- Was too product-oriented vs. solution-oriented.

- Was not responsive to needs.

- Didn't know the industry.

- Was not interested in small business.

- Didn't listen enough.

FIGURE 8-1: **Journey of Transformation for IBM**

Old Paradigm	New Paradigm
Lease Business	Purchase Business
Product-driven	Market-driven
Centralized	Distributed
Control-Oriented	Empowered
Glass House	End User
Contention	Consensus
Hardware Services	Software Services
Low Span of Control	High Span of Control
Generalist	Specialist
5-Year Product Cycles	18-Month Product Cycles

IBM was forced to shift paradigms. Libraries, too, will have to shift many paradigms in the future. What is a paradigm? A paradigm represents a long held custom, belief, or tradition of an organization. To shift paradigms often means that an organization has to change some of the premises that the organization has held to be important.

These paradigm shifts have been very difficult for IBM. But it has managed the shifts through an extensive strategic planning process and employee training. They have become obsessed with customer service. It has focused on teams, enabling employees and becoming market driven. These past few years have been very difficult for IBM. This giant of American industry has been faced with a downturn in sales and profitability and has turned to the tenets of customer service to reverse this trend.

IBM Awards

IBM has a sophisticated reward system with cash bonuses, incentives as well as recognition. One of there rewards is a spontaneous reward that can be copied by libraries. It is called the "JATOMA"—"Just a token of my appreciation." award.

Employees can commend fellow employees with a token of appreciation for when they "catch" the employee providing outstanding customer service. The fact that the token was presented is recorded. The token recipients are publicly acknowledged at staff meetings, and a drawing is held among the recipients for prizes. The prizes might include lunch with the branch manager, or tickets for a play, symphony, or a baseball game. Perhaps, dinner for two—or even a day off. This award is immediate. It encourages good customer service internally within an organization. It is not expensive (prizes can be donated). It makes the staff meetings fun and teaches and reinforces customer service training.

CASE STUDY #2—SOUTHWEST AIRLINES

"The Winning Spirit" Award

Each month a number of employees are selected for the "Winning Spirit" Award. They are given airline passes and featured in the in-house newsletter. They are selected because of their contribution to creating the "Winning Spirit" for the airlines. Southwest Airlines has produced a video on its philosophy of customer service. Its philosophy is based on the belief that it takes a team of employees to create good customer service. And every team member counts if it is to have the winning spirit. For Southwest Airlines, customer service makes the difference between success and failure.

"LUV Committee"

The "LUV Committee" builds team spirit through events and celebrations for the employees. The airline's Houston, Texas, employees host a "Chili Cook-off." The word to all employees is that "It's time to start brushin' up on your mosey'n, cow chip throwin', tobacco spittin', and belt buckle polishin'."

Other events include an annual "pilgrimage" to Athens, Texas. A busload of volunteers go to east Texas for the Muscular Dystrophy Association. These volunteers participate in the yearly summer camp with the kids.

CASE STUDY #3—BEN & JERRY'S—VERMONT'S FINEST ALL-NATURAL ICE CREAM

Seven-and-a-half percent of Ben & Jerry's pre-tax income goes to the Ben & Jerry's Foundation. The Foundation spends its money on a broad array of causes. Employees help make the decision about where the pre-tax income goes. A significant part of their reward system involves assisting the world in which they live.

The company hires the handicapped, provides free therapy sessions—including anonymous free alcohol and drug therapy—to any employee who needs assistance, and takes workers on all-company outings to baseball and hockey games in Montreal. Staff meetings are held once a month in the receiving bay of the Waterbury plant. Production stops so every employee can attend. Coffee and freshly made cider doughnuts are served. Each employee is also allowed to have three pints of ice cream per day.

The "Joy Committee"

This committee was proposed by Jerry. Its role is to serve as the embodiment of Ben & Jerry's spiritual soul. The purpose of the "Joy Committee" is to offset the pressure and demand of growth by keeping the joy in the work environment.

CASE STUDY #4—THE DENVER PUBLIC LIBRARY

This library has several award programs for staff. For example, the Employee of the Year award was established by the Friends of the Library. It recognizes outstanding service by a staff member with a check for $200 and an engraved plaque. Staff members can nominate other staff members. The nominator must provide a description of accomplishments or qualities, that might include, the following: contributions to customer service, leadership, improvement in efficiency of a work unit, personal qualities, initiative, and volunteer activities. The decision about the winner is made by a committee of staff members, human resources, and the Friends.

The Denver Public Library also has a team award. Called the Unit Achievement Award, this award is also made by a nomination from staff members each quarter. A regularly organized work unit or a specially formed group can be recognized. The nominator must indicate staff members participating and describe the project briefly, including objectives and results, and tell how customer service was enhanced.

DEVELOPING YOUR OWN REWARD AND RECOGNITION PROGRAM

When you start to develop a reward and recognition program for your library, it is wise to conduct market research to understand your employees and their needs in terms of reward and recognition. Here is a sample of a survey that can be used to gather significant information. Use the survey to understand your employees' needs and their opinions about appropriate rewards and recognition programs for your library.

FIGURE 8-2: Reward/Recognition Survey

Directions: We who are serving on the staff Reward and Recognition Task Force need your input. Would you please assist us by completing the following survey. Send the survey back to _____ department through interoffice mail.

The information you provide will help us understand your needs in the area of rewards and recognition. This information will be invaluable as we strive to provide the kind of reward programs that build a strong team and encourage individual achievement.

The following is a list of services that are typically recognized by some type of reward in libraries. For each of these services, please indicate your first and second two choices as the most appropriate rewards.

Reward Types

_____ Monetary

_____ Group, Team awards

_____ Individual Recognition

_____ Service pins, book marks, books, gifts

_____ Library Board Recognition

Reason for Reward

_____ Most appropriate

_____ 2nd most appropriate

(continued)

FIGURE 8-2: (Cont.)

Years of service, retirement _____

Service goals reached _____

Program well done _____

Personal achievement on behalf of library _____

Suggestion for improvement for library _____

After each reason, place the number of the reward chosen under the appropriate column.

For each of the services that are rewarded, please indicate from where the reward/recognition should most realistically come. Place the number corresponding to your first and second choices in the appropriate column.

Reward comes from

_____ Manager

_____ Immediate supervisor

_____ Library director

_____ Library board

_____ Executive committee of the library

How often should service recognition be provided? Check appropriate answer.

Every year _____

Every five years _____

Every ten years _____

Upon retirement _____

How would you evaluate the current recognition/reward system at the Library?

Very good _____

Somewhat good _____

Neither good nor bad _____

Somewhat bad _____

Very bad _____

(continued)

FIGURE 8-2: (Cont.)

What are your reasons for evaluating the system the way you do?

_____

_____

What steps should be taken to make the Library more responsive to you and other people in the library like yourself?

_____

_____

The reward and recognition task force "brainstormed" some recognition/reward programs for your consideration. Would you please indicate how you feel about these suggestions by circling the appropriate number. (Rate from 1 to 5, with 1 no good, 5 excellent.)

All staff meetings to recognize jobs well done _____

Sabbaticals _____

Tickets to library events _____

Luncheons, parties _____

Staff luncheons with guest authors _____

Workshops, seminars _____

Professional meetings including ALA, State LA _____

Please give us your comments and ideas.

_____

_____

Please provide us with some personal information:(use appropriate titles for your library)

Job Classification
Shelver (Page)   _____
Clerk   _____
Buildings   _____
Security   _____

(continued)

FIGURE 8-2: (Cont.)

Librarian   _____

Manager   _____

Supervisor   _____

Administrator   _____

Job location   _____

Central library   _____

Branch library   _____

Administration center   _____

Length of service with the library

Under one year   _____

One to five years   _____

Five to ten years   _____

15 to 20 years   _____

More than 20 years   _____

Male _____   Female _____

Use the team approach to develop your reward and recognition system. Reward and recognition programs should be designed to create a sense of teamwork and joy throughout your whole organization. Create a team that is representative. Your team may recommend a variety of awards including years of service, and special team awards. After you implement these reward systems, you should evaluate them on an annual basis. Reward programs become old and stale. Evaluate to make sure that the rewards are actually well received and are meaningful. If they are not, change them.

Money is always an issue. In some libraries, funding for the reward and recognition programs have fit nicely with the goals and objectives of the Friends of the library. The Friends often enjoy providing food and celebration. Their involvement in this process builds a better rapport with the library staff.

The following certificates can be used to reward your employees.

FIGURE 8-3:

You're Super!

A special memo of merit for exceptional service

Date:

To:

From:

_____

_____

_____

_____

_____

_____

_____

_____

_____

_____

_____

_____

FIGURE 8-4:

At Sandstone Public Library

Customers are our #1 concern

The library would like to recognize employees and volunteers who have given you "extra special service." If you have met a special employee, please take a moment to fill out this card.

Name or description:
_____

This staff member is special because:
_____
_____
_____
_____
_____
_____
_____

FIGURE 8-5:

Thank You!

A customer thinks You're Great

To:

Date:

From:

Comment:
_____

_____

FIGURE 8-6:

THANK YOU GRAM

In appreciation of a job well done:

TO: _____ DATE: _____

DEPARTMENT: _____

COMMENTS: _____

_____

_____

_____

_____

_____

_____

FROM: _____

Library Director

FIGURE 8-7:

YOU'RE

A

WINNER

FIGURE 8-8:

TEAMWORK

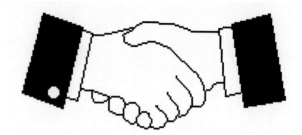

The First Step!

YES!

Wear Your "Teamwork"
T-Shirt on Friday, June 30th
Be a part of the

TEAM

P.S. The director's office has some extra T-shirts

9 MARKET RESEARCH

In order to provide good customer service, we must conduct market research to understand customer needs. What is market research? What are some market research methods that we can use?

When we are looking for information regarding services in other businesses or libraries, we first check various information resources. The resources you will check initially—books, magazines, on-line databases—are all good sources of business information. The information that is already available is still classified as doing market research. However, it is called secondary information—"secondary" because we did not create it, but got it second-hand. Even though it exists, this information, as we well know, can be very difficult to find. When we need information, it is much less expensive to conduct secondary research before we develop our own. Many companies turn to libraries for secondary research purposes.

Information, or research data, that we must obtain in its original form is called primary information. Primary information is the result of original research and is acquired in many ways. When you must have quantitative information you might do written surveys, telephone surveys, personal interviews, mall intercept tests, polling, and so on.

Qualitative information is gathered when you want to know how a specific market segment feels about a product or service. One of the most common ways to acquire qualitative market research is the focus group. A typical focus group consists of approximately 12 individuals who come from the market segment that you wish to target for your products/services. These people are gathered in a room and are led through a discussion by a moderator. The facilitator uses a discussion guide that has been developed in advance to structure the discussion. This group of people may be used to test ideas, concepts, taste-test products, or react to advertising or promotion. Often focus groups are held in a facility with one-way glass so that company executives and marketing staff can see the consumers' reaction immediately. Focus groups provide assistance as you try to understand a specific segment of your marketplace. Focus groups are also very useful in understanding employees as customers.

How do you determine how much to spend on research? What is the cost of a mistake? Market research saves millions of dollars when a company is planning a nation-wide "rollout" of a new consumer product. Market research is "worth it" when it provides data to substantiate budget requests. It is "worth it" when a bond election is pending.

Focus groups usually cost $2500 or more per group. Costs vary depending on incentives that are offered to encourage people to participate. Quantitative studies vary in price depending on methodology and difficulty of study. You can get market research studies donated either on a partial or full basis. These contributions can come from market research companies, corporations that have a market research department, or through marketing departments in local universities.

QUANTITATIVE RESEARCH

MARKET RESEARCH PROVIDES INFORMATION THAT IS THE BASIS FOR BETTER DECISION MAKING

Each year more than a billion dollars is spent in this country for marketing research.

Quantitative studies provide us with statistically accurate information upon which to base decisions. The design of the research project is specific to the information needed and critical to the success of the study.

Should you conduct your own research or pay a market research firm?

FACTORS THAT WILL INFLUENCE THAT DECISION:

1. Economic factors: Can an outside firm provide the information more economically that you can internally?

2. Expertise: Do you have the expertise to conduct the study or obtain the information you need?

3. Special equipment: Does the study program require special equipment or facilities that you do not have? For example, focus groups require a meeting room.

4. Political considerations: Does the study involve controversial issues within the community or library? Studies with political ramifications would generally be conducted by an outside agency.

5. Legal and/or promotional considerations: Will the results of the study be used in legal proceeding or in a promotional campaign—an election, for example. In this case, an outside agency is considered more objective.

6. Administrative facets: Is the current workload of your staff too great to take on one additional study?

7. Confidentiality requirements: Is it absolutely essential that the research by kept secret? As the need for confidentiality increases, the need for using an outside agency decreases.

Research design is the process through which we identify the specific procedures used for collecting and analyzing the data necessary to help identify problems or solve a problem at hand. First of all what specific procedures will enable us to solve the problem? How do we make a decision on the kind of information that needs to be generated? How can we collect data that is relevant to the problem?

STEPS IN THE RESEARCH DESIGN PROCESS

1. Define the research problem.

2. Specify the approximate value of the information. What is the maximum that can be spent on the project? What is the cost of a mistake?

3. Select the data collection method. Will secondary information provide adequate information? Do you need to do a survey? Do you have to have quantitative information? Do you know the appropriate questions to ask? Do you need to do a focus group to better understand the customer in order to develop a quantitative study?

4. Select the measurement technique. Determine whether and how to use questionnaires, attitude scales, observation.

5. Select a sample. Determine who and how many respondents, or objects to measure.

6. Select the analytical approach. Determine the appropriate means of analyzing the data to provide the needed information.

7. Specify the time and financial cost. Develop estimates for each research approach.

8. Prepare the research proposal. Summarize the results of the preceding steps into a proposal.

Example: Your library wants to evaluate developing fee-based services for customers. What are the market research steps that you would take?

1. Defining the research problem: In terms of fee-based services, the research needs are very sophisticated. They include understanding potential customer needs, segmentation analysis, pricing issues, delivery issues, potential demand and competition. These problems represent more than one type of study.

2. The value of the information: Initiating a fee based information service program will require a substantial investment on the part of the library. That investment will be lost unless adequate information is obtained to guide the library in the right direction.

3. Selection of data collection methods: The first step in this process would be to understand how fee based services were operating in other libraries. This information is called secondary information. The information has been produced; it simply must be retrieved. You can retrieve the information through published information, calling other libraries and reviewing other data sources. Understanding potential customer needs will require focus groups. Different segments of potential customers will have different needs. A focus group will provide you with the information necessary to develop a quantitative study. Think about the level of response to a telephone survey or to a written survey. The telephone survey will provide more in-depth information and, perhaps, would be selected on that basis. The quantitative survey will provide you an estimate on the level of demand, pricing issues, and a quantitative analysis of customer needs.

4. Select the measurement technique: In this case, questionnaires were determined to be the measurement of choice.

5. Select the sample: A focus group should consist from 12 to 18 individuals who are from similar segments. A quantitative study, on the other hand, will require a much larger sampling. The actual number depends upon the analysis that we are doing. We want to have a sufficient

number of respondents to provide a statistically accurate response of plus or minus four percent.

6. Select the analytical approach: Who will analyze the data we acquire? Does it require key punching into a computer? How will the analysis be accomplished? When we are dealing with the focus group information, an analysis and report should be developed by the facilitator of the focus group. In the quantitative study, the data will have to be entered into a computer program that has been set up to receive the data and to provide the appropriate analysis. Again, there are outside agencies that do this step, or a university marketing department can contribute this support.

7. Specify the time and financial cost: If we paid outside market research firms to conduct a focus group and to conduct a quantitative study, the costs would be approximately $7,000 to 10,000.

There are four basic measurement techniques used in marketing research:

1. Questionnaires.

2. Attitude scales.

3. Observation.

4. In-depth interviews.

Questionnaires can be handled through telemarketing or through the mail. Each method has positive and negative attributes. The better method is one that provides the most information at the least cost.

Market research budgets are limited for libraries. What kind of market research can you do that is not costly? First of all, walk around the library and talk to customers. Customers are often confused. They do not want to ask and they won't approach a librarian behind a desk easily. Ask if you can help, or ask if they are finding what they need.

Secondly, invite a group of customers in for lunch or for coffee. Ask them what they like about the library, and then ask what you can improve. If you have a particular subject matter, select customers who are interested in that area. Invite customers in frequently and genuinely seek their opinions.

Third, stand in the middle of the library and observe your customers. Observe them using the electronic data bases, and the library's information systems and searching for materials. Ask customers if they are finding what they need.

Here are two versions of an attitude assessment or attitude scale that you can use in your library. Pass one of these forms out to customers within the library. Do this for a set period of

---

FIGURE 9-1: Scale-Based Sample Evaluation

The library has what I need.	+2------------------- 0 --------------- -2
The library does not have what I need.	+2------------------- 0 --------------- -2
Reference services provided the answer.	+2------------------- 0 --------------- -2
I needed.	
The automated catalog is easy to use.	+2------------------- 0 --------------- -2
Materials are easy to find.	+2------------------- 0 --------------- -2
Signage and directions are very helpful.	+2------------------- 0 --------------- -2
Staff is knowledgeable and helpful.	+2------------------- 0 --------------- -2

Demographic information:

Age		Sex M F	Education level
	Under 18		High school
	19-29		Some college
	30-50		College grad
	51-65		Graduate school
	over 65		

time, perhaps over one week. Be sure that you pass these surveys out at various times that the library is open. Pick mornings, evenings, after school, as well as on weekends. Pass out sufficient surveys so that you can see the differences between the responses of young people, adults, and seniors.

You may add other questions. Remember to keep these small surveys very simple. Customers will take the time if they are easy to understand and simple to fill out.

The following is an example of a quantitative study. It is designed to ask customers about their needs for supplies and refreshments at the library. It is provided as an example. These surveys should be distributed and collected at controlled times within the library. The studies returned should represent customers at different times the library is open. You will find a greater demand, perhaps, in the evening or during the lunch hour than at ten in the morning.

FIGURE 9-2:

Question	Strongly agree	Agree	Disagree	Strongly agree
The library has the materials I need.				
It's easy to find the materials.				
Staff are helpful and knowledgeable.				
The computer catalogue is easy to use.				
It is easy to renew books and materials.				
The hours of service are convenient.				
Buildings are clean.				
It is easy to find a place to read and study.				
Demographic Information	Age	Occupation	Library used	Education Level

FIGURE 9-3: Sample Survey Customers' Needs

In an effort to serve you better, the library would like to hear your opinions on the potential new services discussed below. Please take a moment to complete this questionnaire and return it to_____.

General Information:

1. On average, about how often do you visit this library?

    More than once a week............................1

    Once a week....................................2

    Once every two to three weeks...................3

    Once a month..................................4

    Less than once a month.........................5

2. What time of day do you usually visit the library?

    Mornings......................................1

    Afternoons....................................2

    Evenings......................................3

    Varies..4

3. On average, how long do you stay at the library during a typical visit?

    Less than one hour.............................1

    1-2 hours.....................................2

    3-4 hours.....................................3

    Longer than 4 hours...........................4

Food/Beverages:

4. During your visits to this library, do you ever leave the library in order to get something to eat or drink?

    Yes....................1

    No....................2 Skip to Question 6

(continued)

FIGURE 9-3: (Cont.)

5. Considering all the times you visit the library, how often would you say you leave the library to get something to eat or drink?

     Rarely..1

     Occasionally....................................2

     Somewhat frequently...........................3

     Very frequently.................................4

6. The library is considering providing some type of refreshment center within the library building. How interested would you be in having food and beverages available for purchase in the library?

     Very interested...................................1

     Somewhat interested.............................2

     Not at all interested....3 Skip to Question 12

7. Which of the following food items would you like to see in a refreshment center? (Circle all that you are interested in.)

     Candy/cookies/chips...............................1

     Cold sandwiches...................................2

     Hot sandwiches....................................3

     Muffins, rolls, bread items......................4

     Fruit..5

     Beverages such as juices, soda pop, coffee.........6

     Other (please specify)_____

8. How often would you buy food if it was made available through vending machines?

     Never..1

     Rarely...2

     Occasionally.....................................3

     Frequently.......................................4

(continued)

FIGURE 9-3: (Cont.)

9. How often would you buy food if it was served cafeteria style?

Never..1

Rarely...2

Occasionally.......................................3

Frequently...4

10. During which, if any, of the following periods of the day would you purchase food?

10 a.m. to 5 p.m...................................1

5 p.m. to 9 p.m...................................2

11. What other suggestions, if any, do you have for this refreshment center?

_____

_____

Supplies:

12. During your visits to the library, how often do you bring supplies such as pens and paper to use at the library?

Never..1

Seldom...2

Occasionally.......................................3

Frequently...4

13. Have you ever had to leave the library because you ran out of such supplies during your visit?

Yes..1

No...2

(continued)

FIGURE 9-3: (Cont.)

14. How interested would you be in being able to purchase supplies at the library?

    Very interested.......................................1

    Somewhat interested...............................2

    Not at all interested..............................3

15. What type of supplies would you expect the library to sell?
    (Circle all that apply.)

    Pens, pencils and markers...........................1

    Paper...2

    Paper clips..3

    Index cards..4

    Erasers..5

    Typing/word processing supplies.....................6

    Computer discs.......................................7

16. What other supplies would you want to be able to purchase while at the library?

    _____

    _____

17. Do you think the library should offer certain books or manuals for sale?

    Yes...1

    No.................2 Skip to Question 19

18. Which of the following books or manuals would you like to purchase at the library?

    Used books...1

    Dictionaries...2

    Local history publications...........................3

(continued)

FIGURE 9-3: (Cont.)

Test guides..4

Literacy handbooks.................................5

Genealogy handbooks.............................6

Children's books....................................7

19. Do you think the library should offer gifts and library mementos for sale?

Yes......................................1

No.......................................2

20. Which of the following gift items or library mementos would you like to purchase at the library?

Book bags...1

Book marks...2

T-shirts...3

Post cards...4

Thank you for helping us with this survey! Please provide us with some information about your visit to the library.

Date_____

Time_____

Purpose of your visit_____

Department visited_____

Sex....M or F   Age_____

10 IMPLEMENTING YOUR CUSTOMER SERVICE PROGRAM

Libraries and other organizations often implement customer service programs but have disappointing results. Customer service is an institution-wide program that requires the commitment of the library director and administrators. It requires careful planning, the identification of specific people and teams to make it successful, training and more training for staff, as well as on-going monitoring.

Start with the vision of the organization. What is your vision for the library? How do you see it supported? What role should your library play in the community? Clarify the vision, develop a shared vision, keep that vision in sight as you develop your customer service program.

PLANNING

Step 1

Understand your library. How is your library viewed within the community? What are your strengths and weaknesses? How do customers perceive your service as it is now? How do customers feel when they walk into the facility? How are new programs initiated within the library now? How are they received? How responsive have the employees been to new programs? Does the library director "walk around"? Is he or she visible and accessible to employees. What kind of internal communication is going on now? Are his or her memos and in-house newsletters? What kind of reward and recognition program do you have in place at this time? When did you review it last? Are their morale-boosting events, including potluck meals, birthday celebrations, and team competitions? Do the employees participate in decision making processes for the library? Are suggestions and innovations encouraged? Do various departments and branches cooperate for the goodness of the whole? Do people take the initiative or do they say, "It's not in my job description."

Step 2

Understand the employees and their various possible reactions to a customer service plan. Employees will have different reactions to a proposed customer research program. There will be those who are terrific team players. They are willing and able, enthusiastic and supportive. They understand the difference that good service makes. There are also those who are willing but not able. They don't understand what is expected. They don't realize when they are providing inadequate service. Some employees will be resigned. "I will do this if I must." Still another group of employees will be resentful. "This is just another fad. Why don't they really do something about the problems here." There is also the group that considers the program to be an insult. "I'm a professional! You want to train me to smile!"

Step 3

Now that you have reviewed the organization at large as well s the attitudes, values and anticipated behavior of the employees, it is time to develop the best introductory program for your library. Develop communication strategies for each group of employees. Keep in mind that you will be working with all of the employees at once. You cannot separate out the cynics or those who believe that the program is an insult.

Step 4

Identify one individual to serve as the coordinator. This individual needs to be at a position high enough within the organization to command the appropriate respect. You may have to provide a leave of absence from the coordinator's regular job.

Step 5

Conduct customer satisfaction market research studies, if possible, to determine levels of customer satisfaction. Ask specific questions concerning amenities (signage, publications, directions, information), collection, and materials as well as systems within the library. Ask questions concerning the facilities, parking, lighting, adequate space to read and study.

Step 6

Develop a customer service steering committee to work with the coordinator. This committee will be very important to building a broad base of support among the employees as well as those who make the decisions concerning allocation of resources. This committee serves as a problem solving and complaint clearinghouse. It helps prioritize the problems to be examined. It serves to keep the communication devices going to perpetuate the service excellence theme.

After the initial stages of the program, the steering committee serves as a watch dog for the library. It looks for additional issues and problems that affect service excellence. When you establish the service excellence program, you are initiating an ongoing quest to continually improve service. This committee serves to encourage employees and customers alike to assist in the continued march to excellence. This committee also is a sounding board and support system for the service excellence coordinator.

People who should be included on the customer service steering committee include an administrator, the director of human resources, the librarian, perhaps a customer representative, or an individual from the public relations area. There should also be four or five influential employees from different service areas. These people could include, branch and department employees. The chairman of the group can be elected by the group or appointed.

At the first meeting of the committee, invite the participants to share what their personal visions of service excellence are. Outline how this committee will function and the role of the coordinator.

Step 7

Develop an action plan. Identify service objectives, action steps, training needs and time-frame.

IMPLEMENTATION

Step 8

Design a workshop for managers and supervisors. Supervisors and managers are the key to success. These individuals must often change the way they supervise, reprimand, and deal with employees. Provide hands-on training for them. Start this training with case studies in which difficult customer decisions must be made. This training is essential so that supervisors learn how difficult it is to make "informed judgement" decisions. There should be role-playing and problem solving exercises.

Encourage the supervisors to make decision that involve taking risks. The supervisors need to change their thinking before they can help the staff.

The managers within the library setting are the people who are on the front line with employees. They require specific training in order to change their management style to one that empowers employees and encourages good customer service. It is difficult to change the habits of employees who have been employed for 20 years. One workshop will not be enough—but, it is a place to start. Managers need to continue their training with additional workshops and meetings.

Establish objectives including the following:

- To set expectations for consistence customer service

- To set expectations for the manager's role and responsibilities for customer service

- To identify what it is that is needed to meet the expectations of providing consistent customer service.

- To set a plan for implementation of expectations

TRAINING NEEDS FOR MANAGERS TO IDENTIFY

- How to handle customer complaints
- Telephone techniques
- Dealing with disturbed customer
- De-escalating conflict
- Problem-solving
- Using informed judgment
- Use of the automated catalogue
- Reference sources
- Library collection
- Customer service in general
- Others

Step 9

Members of the steering committee should meet with each department or area of the library. The purpose of the meeting is to explain that customer service is everyone's job. The meetings with staff in small numbers create the feeling that every staff member counts. Secondly, it is to determine opportunities within the area to improve service excellence.

Step 10

The steering committee should examine library systems, facilities, amenities and programs from a service excellence perspective. Utilize data from customer satisfaction studies. The steering committee should then identify subcommittees needed to study each of the issues. Those sub-committees should cover the following: New employee orientation, staff development and training, recognition and reward, the employee as a customer. This subcommittee needs to focus on addressing the employees needs for belonging, job enrichment, participation and fun. You may want to call it the "fun" committee. Additional subcommittees should be charged with reviewing performance evaluations, and performance standards. Systems that need to be examined include: library card acquisition, delivery systems, customer information systems, the telephone system, delivery systems, the automated catalog, the reliability of the database, equipment in general, and the accuracy of answers to reference questions. Perhaps you will need to study use of telefax machines.

Chairpersons for the subcommittees can come from the steering committee, or they can be elected by the group. The steering committee should work with the coordinator to appoint members to the subcommittees. They can also come from within the library. Involve employees at all levels on the subcommittees. Subcommittees should the following:

Responsibilities

- Select a chairperson for the group.

- Select a scribe to take notes at meetings.

- Brainstorm appropriate action steps needed to develop necessary recommendations.

- Assign individual responsibilities to members of the task force. People can also work in pairs where appropriate.

- Identify the length of time, amount of research and number of meetings required to develop appropriate recommendations.

- Provide a reporting date to the Steering committee.

- Negotiate any changes or extensions with the Steering committee.

Recommendations:
- Recommendations should reflect improved internal and external customer service.

- Recommendations should include a strong rationale. Any research or fact gathering done by the task force should be itemized and enclosed.

- Recommendations should be presented orally by the subcommittee to the steering committee.

- A written report indicating process followed and recommendations should be produced for administrative staff. The steering committee will make recommendations to the library director.

- Recommendations will often have an impact on budget and staffing levels. Identify in writing sources of revenue to fund recommendations.

- Encourage creative solutions to issues/opportunities.

Step 11
Conduct a meeting with the top management team. This meeting will focus on the role of administrative staff in setting the example of good customer service. Encourage the participation. Ask for their insights into the customer service issues that should be addressed. Focus on leadership training and the importance of role models. Discuss employee resistance and develop methods to encourage change.

Step 12
Kick the program off for the staff with a special all staff meeting. The library director needs to provide the enthusiastic leadership by introducing this program and enforcing the ideals. Present why customer service is so important to the library,

what it will mean to every employee and how it will be rewarding both to the staff and the library.

Focus on the importance of involvement and participation by all of the employees. Indicate that a task force (team) approach will be used to identify specific customer service issue and opportunities. Employees should be actively involved through participation on task forces and in their individual departments.

Step 13
Develop expectations for managers.

1. They should buy-in and be a part of customer service.

2. Managers are responsible for the performance of their staff. If their staff does not perform, they are held accountable.

3. They need to inform staff about what is unacceptable.

4. And they must have the courage to confront inappropriate behavior.

Step 14
Develop expectations for staff. Staffers must do the following:

Understand that there are differences in the concepts of customer service.

Customer service should be fun!

There will be some confusion.

Be willing to do other duties as assigned.

Go beyond what is expected.

Do not withhold information.

Be a model.

Take examples of good customer service to staff meetings.

Reinforce good customer service with other staff members.

Have in-depth discussions with managers for clear interpretations.

Be enthusiastic about being plugged into the plan.

Watch customers eyes light up when you give them good customer service.

Learn how to handle an angry customer.

Be more creative.

Learn to deal with a guide book instead of a rule book.

When faced with a difficult customer service question, bring it to the manager for a discussion.

Realize that it is all right to say "No."

Step 15

Train employees to be workshop leaders. Library employees can be trained to lead service excellence workshops. Here are a few hints that will make this more successful.

1. Choose people from all areas of the library, various levels, departments and positions.

2. Select diverse people by race, ethnic group, gender, and age so that the diversity of your library is reflected.

3. Select people who have the respect and ear of their peers. Look for the informal leaders in your organization.

4. Select people who are good communicators, who have charisma and enthusiasm. Select people who can be role models, who exemplify good customer service.

These workshop leaders should conduct training workshops with every department and group within the library. This peer level work is very effective in buying employees in to the process.

CONTINUING SERVICE EXCELLENCE

Keep the following in mind:

1. The steering committee continues to function. The role of the steering committee becomes one of a watchdog. Members look for additional improvements that can be

made to achieve or maintain service excellence. They monitor market research and performance standards to quantify improvements.

2. Training continues for staff. New employees have an extensive orientation process that is service oriented.

3. The steering committee monitors effectiveness of reward and recognition programs, the work of the "fun" committee and other ongoing projects. Membership on the steering committee should be rotated so that more employees have an opportunity to participate and learn from the experience.

What about the small library? A library that has from three to 50 employees? How do you implement a customer service program?

1. Create an awareness among the staff of the importance of service excellence.

2. Conduct an audit of your current services. Invite a few customers in to talk to you about what you are doing very well and what services could be improved or changed. Form a small committee to address the issues that need improvement or change. Keep asking your customers how you are doing.

3. Conduct staff training. There are a number of good videos available to provide assistance in the training of staff.

4. If there are too few employees to provide formal recognition programs, institute informal recognition programs. Remember that "pat-on-the-back" or a little certificate drawn from the computer can mean a lot.

11 52 WAYS TO KEEP YOUR CUSTOMERS FOR LIFE

1. Create a Service Oriented Culture

Everyone in the library must be customer service oriented. All employees must realize that they work for the customer. Their job is to ensure the ultimate satisfaction of the customer.

2. Have a Service Vision

The service vision is the library's ethic. It is the philosophy of doing business. Everyone must believe and live this vision for the service to be excellent. Management determines the vision, but the staff must make it a reality.

3. Total Involvement

It may be the library director and management that decide to embark on a customer service program, but it is line employees who implement the program. If these employees don't support the initiative, it won't work.

4. Policies in Writing

Put your service policies in writing. However, your employees should have the authority to grant discretionary exceptions to the policies. Policies are only guidelines, and they must be flexible. Employees should be encouraged to use "informed judgement."

5. Employee Empowerment

The employees' job is to satisfy the customer. They need to feel confident in their ability to make decisions on the spot. Support those decisions. Continuous training empowers employees and provides the skills they need to make good decisions.

6. Employee Training

Train, train, train employees. Use case studies within your library. Use examples of actual events. Provide books, seminars, workshops, videos, and group discussions. This training and retraining provides the thread that spreads the library service culture.

Reprinted from Richard Gerson's *Beyond Customer Service*. Copyright © Crisp Publications

7. Promote the Customer Service Program

Promote through library brochures, signs, and displays that you are dedicated to providing superior customer service and that you are interested in customer satisfaction.

8. Hire Good People

Hire people who are well qualified and have good "people" skills.

9. Reward Loyalty

Reward both customers and employees for their loyalty. The rewards must be perceived as valuable by the recipient, but they don't have to cost much money. Sometimes, simple recognition can be a significant reward.

10. Measure the Performance

Those things that get measured get accomplished. If you measure the levels of performance of your staff, you will see an increase in performance levels, quality and productivity. Let everyone know exactly what they must do to provide superior customer service. Make theses standards as objective and measurable as possible. When people achieve these performance levels, customer retention and loyalty naturally follow.

11. Cross Train

Train employees to do other people's jobs. They will be able to provide more assistance to customers and more assistance to each other.

12. Trade Jobs

Have your employees work in other departments. They will develop an appreciation for what other people in the library do. They will also see customer issues and opportunities from a freshness that comes with "being new on the job." Their fresh approach will bring new awareness to customer satisfaction.

13. Establish Easily Accessible Systems

Don't make it hard for customers to work with you. Systems, including public access terminals, the catalogue, renewal systems, book check out systems, and book return systems should all be customer-friendly and easy to use.

14. Call your Library, Establish a Telephone System that Is User Friendly

How many times have you called an office and been totally "turned off" by their telephone system? Ask your customers about your telephone system. Can they get the information they need? Is information accessible by phone when they need it? Are there too many delays? Are customers forwarded from one department to another?

15. Design Flexibility into Your Service Policies

Keep your policies flexible, because each customer and situation is different. Your employees must know that they can modify a written or stated policy to ensure the customers' total satisfaction. You must support your employees' decisions and actions in these situations.

16. Educate the Customer

Use every customer contact to continue to educate your customer about something related to your library. Teach them about new programs and opportunities. They will appreciate it and will continue to do business with you.

17. Handle Complaints Properly

When confronted by an angry customer, acknowledge that the customer is upset. Listen carefully and assure the customer that you are doing everything possible to resolve their complaint. Thank them for bringing the problem to your attention.

18. Develop a Customer Feedback System

Do surveys. Provide customer comment cards at every desk. Solicit customer opinions and comments. Act on customer suggestions. Publicize it when you do act on those suggestions.

20. Every Customer Has a Lifetime Value

Retail companies figure out the value of a customer over a lifetime. Libraries need to keep customers for a lifetime, too.

21. Solicit and Use Employee Ideas

It is your employees who have the daily contact with the customers. They know more about what customers need, expect, and want than managers ever do. Get feedback, ideas, and suggestions from those employees. Implement as many suggestions as possible. Reward good ideas.

22. Be Fair and Consistent

Customers may not always like or agree with what you do for them. You must treat each one fairly and consistently. They will respect you for it.

23. Underpromise and Overdeliver

When you overpromise and can't deliver, the customer goes away disappointed. If you set realistic expectations for the customer based on your level of service and then exceed those expectations, the customer is more than satisfied.

24. Remember, It Is the Benefits of the Service That Are Important to the Customer.

We tend to think about the features of the library and forget that our customers come for the benefits. One "benefit" to customers is that they can find the information they need to solve a problem. Easy access, systems that work, helpful staff members make it easier for customers to get the necessary benefits.

25. High Touch As Well As High Tech

Libraries are becoming more and more technologically oriented. Public access terminals, on-line data bases, automated catalogues, reader-printers—the list goes on and on. Library staff members must learn to be facilitators assisting the customer with the high tech. Libraries will become the "warm fuzzy" information access point.

26. Ask Customers What They Want

Constantly ask customers what they need from you and what you can do for them. Walk about, ask customers in your library.

27. Service Management on a Daily Basis

Ask your employees what would make their jobs easier. Treat your employees as customers. If there are problems, make the necessary adjustments and resolve them quickly.

28. Realize the Cost of Losing a Customer

Grocers realize that one customer can mean $5000 a year in sales. When you consider that every unhappy customer tells 11 other people, the loss can be sizable. Realize that the cost of losing a customer results in a lost donor, voter, or supporter.

29. Know Your Competition

Libraries have a great deal of competition—competition for funds, competition for programs and services. Excellent customer service can propel you ahead of the competition and "position" the library as a vital and necessary community service.

30. Conduct Market Research

You can never have enough information about your customers. Do surveys, interviews, focus groups, whatever it takes to understand customer needs. Then adapt your services to meet customers needs.

31. Know What Your Customers Need, Want, and Expect

Find out what customers want, need and expect and then give it to them. Remember that customers needs change. Change with them.

32. Find, Nurture and Display Customer Champions

Every library has one, two, or several employees who are true customer champions. Find out who these people are, nurture and support them, and make them role models for everyone else to follow. Reward the behavior.

33. Communication Is Critical

Train employees in communication skills. Telephone skills as well as personal skills with customers. Train them how to listen first and develop rapport with the customers.

34. Smile

Smiling makes employees feel good. It makes customers feel good as well.

35. Make Customers Feel Important

Call customers by name. Ask them about themselves. Get to know their favorite authors and subject matter. Your reward will be a lifetime customer.

36. Promote Your Customers

Use your customers in your promotion pieces, annual reports, events. Let them tell their story to other potential customers, politicians, and the press. This endorsement fosters credibility. Your customers will enjoy being involved.

37. Create Customer Advisory Groups

You can form advisory groups for several different areas. Have these advisors work with you to understand customer needs.

38. Strive for Excellence

If you expect average service, that is what you will get. However, if you expect excellence, your employees will work to provide excellence.

39. Employees Are customers, Too.

Internal customer relations is every bit as important as external customer service. Employees should provide the same level of service for each other as they do for customers.

40. Let Customers Know You Care

Send customers, donors, supporters, and volunteers thank you cards, holiday cards, and anything else that is appropriate to let them know you care.

41. Make Service Results Visible

Post your customer comment cards and letters for all customers to see. Post employee rewards and commendations for all to see. Make service results visible.

42. Go the Extra Mile

Call the customer when their reserve book is in. Deliver the information within 24 hours. Provide the extra service you would like to receive.

43. Develop Reward and Recognition Programs for Staff

Not all rewards need to be monetary. Sometimes, simple recognition is a great reward. Develop reward programs that can be awarded quickly and on the spot.

44. Give Your People a Break

Customer contact work can be very emotionally demanding. People need breaks to stay sharp and do it right.

45. Develop a Theme and Get Everyone Involved

Federal Express says, *"Absolutely, positively anywhere overnight!"* This short theme is easily remembered and quoted by both employees and customers. Find a theme for your service too. It needs to be short, succinct, and descriptive of your uniqueness.

46. Disarm the Chronic Complainer

Every organization has the chronic complainer. While they are fortunately rare, they can require a lot of time and patience. When confronted with a chronic complainer, try these techniques:

Active listening. Identify the legitimate grievance beneath the griping. Restate the problem and confirm the issue. Establish the facts.

Resist the temptation to apologize. Often complainers are trying to fix blame instead of solve problems. Encourage the complainer to pose solutions. Often you must put a time limit on the conversation.

47. Use Hoopla and Fun

Excellent libraries are fun places to work! They create rituals. They celebrate birthdays, special events, and special days.

48. Fish for Negative Feedback

Complaining customers can be your best friends. Without their complaints, we would not know how to improve. Design systems to receive those complaints. Let customers know that you want their honest opinions.

49. Enjoy People and Their Diversity

Library customers come in all shapes, sizes, colors, and ages. Every person is different and unique. Enjoy the diversity. Avoid saying anything negative or judgmental about another person.

50. Watch Personal Appearance and Grooming

Dress appropriately. Managers should set the example for staff. Look around you and see what the customer sees. Are the books well displayed? Is the library clean? Are the restrooms clean?

51. Create a Comfortable Physical Environment

Are there comfortable chairs? Is the lighting adequate to read and study by? Is the signage adequate? Have books been placed back on the shelves so that other customers can find them? Are there displays that create an attractive area?

52. Speak English Not "Libraryese"

Libraries are full of acronyms. It is easy to discuss PAC terminals, CARL systems, on-line databases, and various other acronyms. Remember, your customers don't know those terms!

BIBLIOGRAPHY

Albrecht, Karl. *At America's Service: How Corporations Can Revolutionize the Way They Treat Their Customers*. Homewood, IL: Business 1 Irwin, 1988.

Albrecht, Karl and Ron Zemke. *Service America! Doing Business in the New Economy*. New York: Warner Book, Inc., 1985.

Anderson, Kristin and Ron Zemke. *Delivering Knock Your Socks Off Service*. New York: AMACOM, 1991.

The BBP Customer Service Management Handbook, Bureau of Business Practice, Waterford, CT.

Bender, Paul S. *Design and Operation of Customer Service Systems*.

Bleuel, William H. and J. D. Patton, Jr. *Service Management: Principles and Practices*, 2nd ed. Research Triangle Park, NC: Instrument Society of America, 1986.

Davidow, William, H. *Total Customer Service: The Ultimate Weapon*. New York: HarperCollins, 1990.

Desatnick, Robert L. *Managing to Keep the Customer: How To Achieve & Maintain Superior Customer Service Troughout the Organization*. San Francisco: Jossey-Bass, 1987.

Desatnick, Robert L. *Keep the Customer! Making Customer Service Your Competitive Edge*. Boston: Houghton Mifflin, 1990.

Cannie, Joan Koob. *Keeping Customers for Life*. New York: AMACOM, 1990.

Carr, Clay. *Front Line Customer Service: 15 Keys to Customer Satisfaction*. New York: John Wiley and Sons, Inc., 1990.

Finch, Lloyd C. *Telephone Courtesy & Customer Service*. Los Altos, CA: Crisp Publications, 1990.

Fromm, Bill. *The Ten Commandments of Business and How to Break Them*. New York: Berkley Publishing, 1992

Ford, Lisa. *How to Give Exceptional Customer Service*. 2-set videotape. Boulder (CO): Career Track Publications, c: 1989.

Gerson, Richard. *Beyond Customer Service*. Menlow Park, CA: Crisp Publications, 1992

Glen, Peter. *It's Not My Department.* (Sound recording) 1992.

Goldzimer, Linda Silverman, with Gregory L. Beckmann. *"I'm First—" Your Customer's Message to You.* New York: Berkley Publishing Group , 1989.

Gregory, Helen H. *Finding and Keeping Customers: A Small Business Handbook.* Sedro Woolley, WA: Pinstripe Publishing, 1989.

Hanan, Mack, and Peter Karp. *Customer Satisfaction: How to Maximize, Measure, and Market Your Company's Ultimate Product.* New York: AMACOM, 1989.

Heskett, James L. *Service Breakthroughs: Changing the Rules of the Game.* New York: Macmillan, 1990.

Hopkins, David. *Customer Service: A Progress Report.*

Kausen, Robert C. *Customer Satisfaction Guaranteed: A New Approach to Customer Service.* Trinity Center, CA: Life Education, Inc., 1989.

Lash, Linda. *The Complete Guide to Customer Service.* New York: John Wiley and Sons, Inc., 1989.

LeBoeuf, Michael. *How to Win Customers and Keep Them for Life.* New York: Berkley Publishing, 1989.

Leebov, Wendy, Ed. D. *Service Excellence: The Customer Relations Strategy for Health Care.* Chicago: American Hospital Publishing, Inc., 1988.

Liswood, Laura A., 	*Serving Them Right: Innovative and Powerful Customer Retention Strategies.* New York: HarperCollins 1990.

Martin, William B. *Quality Customer Service: The Art of Treating Customers as Guests.* Crisp Publications, Inc.: Los Altos, CA, 1989.

Moseley, Lloyd W. *Customer Service: The Road To Greater Profits.*

National Association of Service Managers. *The Management of Change.*

Peters, Thomas J. and Robert H. Waterman, Jr. *In Search of Excellence: Lessons from America.* New York: HarperCollins, 1982.

Peters, Thomas J. and Nancy K. Austin. *Passion for Excellence: The Leadership Difference.* New York: Random House, 1985.

Sewell, Carl and Paul B. Brown. *Customers for Life: How to Turn That One-Time Buyer into a Lifetime Customer.* New York: Doubleday, 1990.

Sonnenberg, Frank K. *Marketing to Win: Strategies for Building Competitive Advantage in Service Industries.* New York: Harper Business, 1990.

Spechler, Jay. *When America Does It Right: Case Studies in Service Quality.* Norcross, GA: Industrial Engineering & Management Press, 1948.

White, Jack M. *The Angry Buyer's Complaint Directory.*

Wilson, Jerry R. *Word-of-Mouth Marketing.* New York: John Wiley & Sons, Inc.: 1991.

Zeithaml, Valarie A. *Delivering Quality Service: Balancing Customer Perceptions and Expectations.* New York: Free Press, 1990.

Zemke, Ron. *The Service Edge: 101 Companies That Profit from Customer Care.* New York: NAL-Dutton, 1990.

INDEX